Air Fryer Cookbook UK

Crispy & Tasty recipes to enjoy with friends & family

by Megan J. Walker

© Copyright 2022 by Megan J. Walker - All rights reserved.

This paper is geared towards providing exact and reliable information regarding the topic and issue at hand. The publication is sold with the idea that the publisher is not required to render accounting, officially permitted, or otherwise, qualified services. If advice, legal or professional, is needed, you should seek the advice of a person experienced in the profession.

From a statement of principles that has been accepted and approved equally by a committee of the American Bar Association and a committee of publishers and associations.
It is not legal in any way to reproduce, duplicate, or transmit any part of this document in either electronic or printed media. Recording of this publication is strictly prohibited, and any storage of this document is not permitted except with the written permission of the publisher. All rights reserved. The information provided herein is stated to be true and consistent, in that any liability, in terms of inattention or otherwise, for any use or misuse of any policy, process, or direction contained within is the sole and Total responsibility of the receiving reader. Under no circumstances will any legal liability or fault be held against the publisher for any repair, damage, or monetary loss due to the in- formation contained herein, either directly or indirectly.

The respective authors own all copyrights not held by the publisher.
The information contained herein is offered for informational purposes only and is universal as such. The presentation of the information is without contract or any type of warranty assurance. Trademarks used are without consent, and publication of the trademark is without permission or endorsement from the trademark owner. All trademarks and brands within this book are for clarification purposes only and are the property of the owners themselves, not affiliated with this document.

DISCLAIMER
The information contained in the Book is for informational purposes only, and in no way constitutes the making of a diagnosis or prescription for treatment.
The information contained in this book is not intended and should not in any way replace the direct relationship doctor-patient or specialist examination.
It is recommended that you always seek the advice of your physician and/or specialists for any reported indication.

INTRODUCTION 10

How does an air fryer work? 10

How to Use Your Air fryer 11

Health Benefits of Air Fryers 11

BREAKFAST RECIPE 13

- Egg White Greek Omelet — 13
- Spicy Cabbage — 13
- Zucchini Noodles — 14
- Red pepper frittata — 14
- Rice, Almonds and Raisins Pudding — 15
- Turkey Burrito — 16
- Oatmeal Casserole — 16
- Vegan Air Fryer Garlic Bread — 17
- Cherries Risotto — 18
- Shrimp Sandwiches — 18
- Cinnamon Cream Cheese Oats — 19
- Mushroom Quiche — 20

Air Fried Tofu Breakfast 21

Breakfast Pea Tortilla 21

Ham Breakfast Pie 22

Blackberry French Toast 22

Beans and Egg Breakfast Mix 23

Okra and Corn Salad 24

APPETIZER AND SNACKS 25

Air Fryer Carrot Fries 25

Coconut Chicken Bites 25

Air Fryer Jalapeno Poppers 26

Shrimp Muffins 26

Stuffed Peppers 27

Zucchini Cakes 27

Pumpkin Muffins 28

Stuffed Tomatoes With Spinach And Cheese 29

Buffalo Cauliflower Snack 29

Roasted Garlic 30

Empanadas ... 30

Spinach Balls ... 31

VEGETARIAN RECIPE 32

Eggplant and Zucchini Mix ... 32

Air Fried Broccoli Salad Broccoli ... 32

Roasted Asparagus ... 33

Tomato and Basil Tart ... 33

Stuffed Tomatoes ... 34

Brussels Sprouts and Butter Sauce ... 34

Tomatoes and Bell Pepper Sauce ... 35

Crispy Potatoes and Parsley ... 35

Turnips Salad ... 36

Broccoli Crust Pizza ... 36

Baked Crispy Avocado Tacos ... 37

Air Fryer Green Beans ... 38

FISH AND SEAFOOD 39

Air Fryer Lobster Tails with Lemon-Garlic Butter ... 39

Air Fried Salmon Cakes 39

Air Fryer White Fish with Garlic 40

Air Fryer Lemon Pepper Shrimp 41

Red Snapper 41

Swordfish and Mango Salsa 42

Air Fried Salmon 42

Air Fry Crunchy Cod Fillets 43

Air Fried Scallops 44

Air Fried Shrimp 44

Air-Fried Shrimp Fajitas 45

POULTRY RECIPE 46

Air Fryer Shredded Chicken 46

Paleo Baked Chicken Nuggets in the Air Fryer 46

Best Air Fryer Chicken Fajitas Recipe 47

Air Fryer Lemon Pepper Wings 48

Air Fryer Cheesy Bacon Hasselback Chicken 49

Chicken and Black Olives Sauce 49

Broccoli Cheddar Chicken Fritters 50

Chinese Stuffed Chicken 51

Chicken Parmesan 51

Chicken and Garlic Sauce 52

BEEF RECIPE 53

Air Fryer Marinated Flank Steak 53

Air Fryer Roast Beef 53

Crispy Beef and Broccoli Stir-Fry 54

Classic Mini Meatloaf 55

Keto Meatballs With Almond Flour 56

Tender Air Fryer Steak with Garlic Mushrooms 57

Garlic and Bell Pepper Beef 57

Flavored Rib Eye Steak 58

Steaks and Scallops 59

Chorizo and Beef Burger 59

Greek Beef Meatballs Salad 60

PORK AND LAMB RECIPE 62

Easy Air Fryer Pork Chops … 62

Air Fryer Sausage … 62

Air Fryer Honey Mustard Pork Chops … 63

Marinated Pork Chops and Onions … 64

Pork Chops and Green Beans … 64

Pulled Pork … 65

Lamb and Spinach Mix … 65

Air Fryer Lamb Meatballs … 66

Lamb Roast and Potatoes … 67

Easy Lamb Kofta … 67

DESSERT RECIPE 69

Chocolate Cookies … 69

Pecan Brownies … 69

Chocolate Espresso Mini Cheesecake … 70

Coconut Flour Mug Cake … 70

Toasted Coconut Flakes … 71

Vanilla Pound Cake … 72

Raspberry Danish Bites … 72

Pumpkin Cookies … 73

Lime Cheesecake … 73

Easy Granola … 74

SIDE RECIPE 75

Herbed Tomatoes … 75

Eggplant Side Dish … 75

Onion Rings Side Dish … 76

Corn with Lime and Cheese … 76

Potato Wedges … 77

INTRODUCTION

The air fryer simplifies the preparation of delightful, healthy meals. To prepare meals, the device uses swift hot air circulation rather than heated fat and oil, which can be harmful to your health. The technique ensures that the food's surface is crispy and the interior is well cooked.

Using the air fryer, we can cook a broad variety of dishes and practically anything. The tower air fryer can cook a broad range of items, including meat, vegetables, poultry, fruits, fish, and a variety of desserts. You may prepare everything from the appetizers through the main course and dessert. Not to mention that the tower air fryer allows you to make wonderful cakes, desserts, and handmade preserves.

How does an air fryer work?

The look of an air fryer may differ depending on the brand, size, and price. However, there are a few components to be aware of, namely:
- a heating element
- a fan
- a drawer where the food is placed
- the controls, which are normally located on the front of the air fryer
- a basket or grating that lifts and retains the food contained within the drawer

You can better understand how the air fryer works if you are aware of these components.

The cooking process

To begin, it is essential to understand that an air fryer does not properly cook your food. When food is fried, it is cooked in hot oil by definition. Although frying involves the use of oil, you may shallow fry in a pan or deep fry in a skillet with the oil around the food.

In theory, an air fryer is similar to a deep fryer in that the heat source completely envelops the food and touches its whole surface area at once (in the case of deep frying, hot oil). Deep frying provides quickly crispy food since the item absorbs strong heat all at once.

The air fryer, like a convection oven, cooks food. After setting the temperature, you place the meal in the cooking drawer. The fan circulates the hot air produced by the heating element swiftly.

How to Use Your Air fryer

1. The air fryer must be warmed before it can be used to cook. When the air fryer is warmed, the food will cook faster and have a crisper outside. You may quickly warm a multi-function gadget by pressing the preheat button. You will, however, need to manually warm small, low-cost air fryers. Turn on the air fryer for five minutes at 204°C for manual preheating.
2. After the air fryer has finished preheating, remove the air fryer basket and add the food. However, keep in mind that putting too much food in the basket may result in the meal not being cooked properly.
3. After filling the air fryer basket with food, place it into the air fryer. Establish the proper temperature and time for meals next. You may, however, change the temperature and length during cooking.
4. Press the start button to begin air frying. After you start cooking, you must keep an eye on the meal to ensure it is neither overcooked or burnt. To guarantee that the meal is cooked, mix the ingredients while it is cooking or turn the food upside down. When the cooking time is up, the air fryer will beep.
5. After that, remove the air fryer basket. But be cautious of the steam's heat. After separating the inner and outer baskets, serve the meal. While separating the inner and outer baskets, keep the basket on a level surface. The basket must be totally cold before cleaning.

Health Benefits of Air Fryers

Reduce your fat and calorie consumption
Let's start with the basics. An air fryer's built-in high-speed fans disperse air uniformly while crisping up food with a thin layer of oil. Because it does not utilize additional oils, this gadget makes your meals healthier, allowing you to maintain an active lifestyle without sacrificing your appetite.
It's simple to enjoy tasty meals without adding extra calories to your diet with an air fryer. Many studies show that using an air fryer to make food reduces the quantity of fat by 50 times, resulting in a meal with much fewer calories and fat.

It allows you to preserve more nutrients in your diet.
You'll be relieved to find that air fryers can retain nutrients such as Vitamin C and polyphenols, which are generally lost during traditional cooking techniques. They don't just provide a crunchy texture and taste. Air fryers use less heat than traditional ovens, allowing food to retain more of its nutritional content and natural flavor. This is especially important for antioxidant-rich diets like fruits and vegetables. Using this

culinary utensil will add crunch and taste to your food while retaining the nutritious benefits of a home-cooked meal.

The use of an air fryer does not interfere with your diet.

An air fryer is a good way to cut calories and fat when cooking. It uses far less oil than traditional methods of cooking, allowing you to enjoy gourmet meals without jeopardizing your weight-loss efforts.

The food made in an air fryer may reduce your calorie consumption, assisting in weight reduction. It just requires a thin coating or a few drops of oil, so you may fulfill your desires while limiting your saturated fat intake.

Safer Cooking

One of the benefits of utilizing an air fryer is that it cooks faster and safer. This equipment uses less oil and is far safer than traditional cooking methods. It suggests that you will not consume extra fat, which might increase your risk of heart disease and other health problems.

Furthermore, because air frying takes less time than baking or broiling, you may cook more food in the same amount of time. As a result, it's an excellent choice for people who are pressed for time and don't have time to wait for their meal to cook.

Reduced Energy Consumption

Air fryers use less energy than traditional cooking methods such as stovetop or oven cooking and do not need to be heated or cooled. Furthermore, it does not emit any harmful smoke or fumes, which is another concern linked with frying on a stovetop or in an oven.

BREAKFAST RECIPE

Egg White Greek Omelet

Preparation time: 10 minutes
Cooking time: 15 minutes
Servings: 4

Ingredients:
- 223 grams of egg whites
- 50 g sliced tomato
- 30 ml skim milk
- 25 g sliced mushrooms
- 6 g chopped chives
- To taste, season with salt and black pepper.

Preparation
1. Combine egg whites, tomato, milk, mushrooms, chives, salt, and pepper in a mixing dish, then pour into the pan of your air fryer.
2. Cook for 15 minutes at 160°C, then cool, slice, divide among plates, and serve.
3. Enjoy!

Nutritional information: calories 100, fat 3g, fiber 6g, carbs 7g, carbs 4g

Spicy Cabbage

Preparation time: 10 minutes
Cooking time: 8 minutes
Servings: 4

Ingredients:
- 1 cabbage, divided into 8 wedges
- Sesame seed oil (15 mL)
- 1 grated carrot
- Apple cider vinegar, 60 mL
- Apple juice (60 mL)
- 2.5 ml cayenne pepper
- 5 mL crushed red pepper flakes

Preparation
1. In a pan that fits your air fryer, combine cabbage, oil, carrot, vinegar, apple juice, cayenne pepper, and pepper flakes, mix, and cook at 176 degrees C for 8 minutes.

2. Dish up the cabbage mixture.

Nutritional information: calories 100, fat 4g, fiber 2g, carbs 11g, protein 7g

Zucchini Noodles

Preparation time: 10 minutes
Cooking time: 20 minutes
Servings: 6

Ingredients:
- 30 milliliters olive oil
- 3 zucchini slices spiralized
- 454 g sliced mushrooms
- 14 g sun-dried tomatoes diced
- 3 g minced garlic
- 114 g halved cherry tomatoes
- 450 g sauce de tomates
- 60 g torn spinach
- To taste, salt and black pepper.
- a handful of chopped basil

Preparation
1. Set aside for 10 minutes after seasoning the zucchini noodles with salt and black pepper.
2. In a pan that fits your air fryer, heat the oil over medium-high heat, add the garlic, stir, and cook for 1 minute.
3. Stir in the mushrooms, sun-dried tomatoes, cherry tomatoes, spinach, cayenne pepper sauce, and zucchini noodles before placing in the air fryer for 10 minutes at 160° C.
4. Serve on plates, topped with a dusting of basil.

Nutritional information: calories 120, fat 1g, fiber 1g, carbs 2g, protein 9g

Red pepper frittata

Preparation time: 10mins
Cooking time: 15mins
Servings: 2

Ingredients
- 6 medium British Lion eggs
- 1 large red pepper
- 1 small white onion
- 2 new potatoes
- 1 large handful of Gruyere cheese or mature Cheddar cheese
- Salt and pepper to season

Preparation

1. Preheat the airfryer to 200° Celsius.
2. In a saucepan, boil the raw potatoes until they are soft (you should be able to put a knife through them easily).
3. In the meantime, finely chop the onion, grate the cheese, and cut the peppers.
4. Season the eggs with salt and pepper to taste.
5. Heat a small quantity of oil in a frying pan with a metal handle (very important). Cook for approximately 5 minutes on medium to low heat, or until the onions and peppers are soft.
6. When the potatoes are tender, drain them and evenly distribute them in the pan.
7. Immediately add the eggs, followed by the cheese. Allow for a few minutes of cooking before placing the pan in the airfryer to complete cooking. This should take no more than five minutes, and the top should be golden brown.
8. Remove the frittata from the airfryer with caution (remember the metal handle) and let aside for a few minutes to enable it to settle before delicately turning it out onto a plate.
9. It works great with a tomato and red onion salad and may be served hot or cold. It's certainly worth a go, and it only takes 25 minutes to make..

Nutritional information: calories 189, Carbs 14g, Fat 9.9g, Protein 12g.

Rice , Almonds and Raisins Pudding

Preparation time: 5 minutes
Cooking time: 8 minutes
Servings: 4

Ingredients:

- brown rice (202 g)
- Coconut chips (37 g)
- 237 mL of milk
- 473 mL bottled water
- 118 milliliters maple syrup
- 40 grams raisins
- almonds (36 g)
- 5 ml cinnamon powder

Preparation

1. Put the rice in a pan that fits your air fryer, fill with water, and cook over medium high heat until the rice is tender. Drain.
2. Combine the milk, coconut chips, almonds, raisins, cinnamon, and maple syrup in a mixing bowl. Cook for 8 minutes at 182 degrees Celsius in an air fryer.
3. Rice pudding should be served in separate servings.

Nutritional information: calories 251, fat 6g, fiber 8g, carbs 39g, protein 12g

Turkey Burrito

Preparation time: 10 minutes
Cooking time: 10 minutes
Servings: 2

Ingredients:
- 4 slices turkey breast already cooked
- ½ red bell pepper, sliced
- 2 eggs
- 1 small avocado, peeled, pitted and sliced
- 36 g salsa
- Salt and black pepper to the taste
- 225 g mozzarella cheese, grated
- Tortillas for serving

Preparation
1. In a mixing bowl, whisk the eggs with salt and pepper to taste, then pour them into a pan and set it in the air fryer basket.
2. Cook for 5 minutes at 204°C before removing pan from fryer and placing eggs on a platter.
3. Distribute the eggs, turkey meat, bell pepper, cheese, salsa, and avocado among the tortillas on a work surface.
4. Roll your burritos and lay them in an air fryer coated with tin foil.
5. Heat the burritos for 3 minutes at 149° C before dividing them onto plates and serving.

Nutritional information: calories 349, fat 23g, fiber 11g, carbs 20g, protein 21g

Oatmeal Casserole

Preparation time: 10 minutes
Cooking time: 20 minutes
Servings: 8

Ingredients:
- 2 cups oats, rolled
- 4 mL baking soda
- brown sugar (67 g)

- Cinnamon powder, 5 mL
- Chocolate chips (80 g)
- Blueberries (65 g)
- 1 peeled and mashed banana
- 473 mL of milk
- 1 eggs
- 28 g of butter
- 5 milliliters vanilla extract
- Spray cooking oil

Preparation

1. In a mixing bowl, combine the sugar, baking powder, cinnamon, chocolate chips, blueberries, and banana.
2. Whisk together the eggs, vanilla extract, and butter in a separate bowl.
3. Preheat your air fryer to 160°C, then coat the bottom with frying spray and layer with oats.
4. Cook for 20 minutes after adding the cinnamon-egg mixture.
5. Before dividing into dishes and dishing for breakfast, give it one last good stir.

Nutritional information: calories 300, fat 4g, fiber 7g, carbs 12g, protein 10g

Vegan Air Fryer Garlic Bread

Preparation time 3 mins
Cooking time 5 mins
Total time 8 mins
Servings 4

Ingredients

- 4 mini flour tortillas
- 56 g vegan butter (or vegan spread)
- 2 large cloves of garlic
- 1.25 ml dried parsley (or fresh, chopped)
- 1 generous pinch of chilli flakes
- 1 pinch salt and pepper

Preparation

1. Peel and smash the garlic, or grate it coarsely.
2. Soften the butter in a basin using the back of a spoon.

3. After adding the garlic, herbs, and chili, season with salt and pepper.
4. Thoroughly combine.
5. Distribute the mixture evenly across four mini flour tortillas.
6. In an air fryer, bake for 5 minutes at 180°C. Keep an eye on it, and if you have shelves, change them out since the top one cooks quicker.
7. Before serving, cut into triangles.

Nutritional information: Calories: 88kcal Carbohydrates: 1g Protein: 0.2g Fat: 9g

Cherries Risotto

Preparation time: 10 minutes
Cooking time: 12 minutes
Servings: 4

Ingredients:
- Arborio rice (301 g)
- cinnamon powder (7.5 mL)
- Brown sugar (65 g)
- a pinch of salt
- 28 g of butter
- 2 cored and sliced apples
- Juice 237 mL
- 707 mL of milk
- 80 g dried cherries

Preparation
1. Heat the butter in a skillet that fits your air fryer over medium heat, then add the rice, stir, and cook for 4-5 minutes.
2. Stir in the sugar, apples, apple juice, milk, cinnamon, and cherries. Place in the air fryer and cook at 176° C for 8 minutes.
3. Divide the mixture into dishes and serve for breakfast.

Nutritional information: calories 162, fat 12g, fiber 6g, carbs 23g, protein 8g

Shrimp Sandwiches

Preparation time: 10 minutes
Cooking time: 5 minutes
Servings: 4

Ingredients:
- 170 g canned small shrimp, drained
- 176 g cheddar, shredded
- mayonnaise (43 g)
- 11 g chopped green onions
- 4 whole wheat bread pieces
- 28 g softened butter

Preparation
1. Combine the shrimp, cheddar, green onion, and mayo in a mixing dish.
2. Spread half of the bread pieces with this, then top with the remaining bread slices, cut in half diagonally and spread with butter.
3. Cook the sandwiches in the air fryer for 5 minutes at 176° C.
4. Plate the shrimp sandwiches for breakfast.

Nutritional information: calories 162, fat 3g, fiber 7g, carbs 12g, protein 4g

Cinnamon Cream Cheese Oats

Preparation time: 10 minutes
Cooking time: 25 minutes
Servings: 4

Ingredients:
- Steel oats (160 g)
- 710 mL of milk
- 14 g of butter
- 119 grams raisins
- Cinnamon powder, 5 mL
- Brown sugar (50 g)
- White sugar (25 g)
- 57 g cream cheese

Preparation

1. Heat the butter in a skillet that fits your air fryer over medium heat, then add the oats, mix, and toast for 3 minutes.
2. Stir in the milk and raisins, then place in the air fryer and cook at 182 degrees Celsius for 20 minutes.
3. Meanwhile, combine cinnamon and brown sugar in a mixing dish and whisk to combine.
4. In a separate dish, stir together white sugar and cream cheese.
5. Divide the oats among the bowls and top with cinnamon and cream cheese.

Nutritional information: calories 152, fat 6g, fiber 6g, carbs 25g, protein 7g

Mushroom Quiche

Preparation time: 10 minutes
Cooking time: 10 minutes
Servings: 4

Ingredients:

- 17 ml flour
- 14 g butter, soft
- 9 inch pie dough
- 2 button mushrooms, chopped
- 37 g ham, chopped
- 3 eggs
- 1 small yellow onion, chopped
- 76 g heavy cream
- A pinch of nutmeg, ground
- Salt and black pepper to the taste
- 2.5 ml thyme, dried
- 56 g Swiss cheese, grated

Preparation

1. Flour your work surface and roll out the pie dough.
2. Press it into the bottom of your air fryer's pie plate.
3. Whisk together the butter, mushrooms, ham, onion, eggs, heavy cream, salt, pepper, thyme, and nutmeg in a mixing bowl.
4. Spread this over the pie shell, then top with Swiss cheese and set in the air fryer.
5. Cook your quiche for 10 minutes at 204 degrees C.

6. Cut into slices and serve for breakfast.

Nutritional information: calories 212, fat 4g, fiber 6g, carbs 7g, protein 7g

Air Fried Tofu Breakfast

Preparation time: 10 minutes
Cooking time: 12 minutes
Servings: 2

Ingredients:
- 1 tofu block, pressed and cubed
- Salt and black pepper to the taste
- 6.8 g smoked paprika
- 30 g cornstarch
- Cooking spray

Preparation
1. Cooking spray the air fryer basket and heat the fryer to 187 degrees C.
2. Toss tofu with salt, pepper, smoked paprika, and cornstarch in a mixing bowl.
3. Cook for 12 minutes, stirring the fryer every 4 minutes, with tofu in the basket of your air fryer.

Nutritional information: calories 172, fat 4g, fiber 7g, carbs 12g, protein 4g

Breakfast Pea Tortilla

Preparation time: 10 minutes
Cooking time: 7 minutes
Servings: 8

Ingredients:
- 454 g baby peas
- 57 g butter
- 367 g yogurt
- 8 eggs
- 13 g mint, chopped
- Salt and black pepper to the taste

Preparation

1. In a pan large enough to fit your air fryer, melt the butter over medium heat, then add the peas, stir, and cook for a few minutes.
2. Meanwhile, in a mixing dish, combine half of the yoghurt, salt, pepper, eggs, and mint.
3. Pour this over the peas, mix, and cook for 7 minutes at 176° C in your air fryer.
4. Spread the remaining yoghurt on top of the tortilla and serve.

Nutritional information: calories 192, fat 5g, fiber 4g, carbs 8g, protein 7g

Ham Breakfast Pie

Preparation time: 10 minutes
Cooking time: 25 minutes
Servings: 6

Ingredients:

- 453 g crescent rolls dough
- 2 eggs, whisked
- 470 g cheddar cheese, grated
- 15 g parmesan, grated
- 135 g cooked and chopped
- Salt and black pepper to the taste
- Cooking spray

Preparation

1. Preheat your air fryer to 176°C and coat it with frying spray.
2. Whisk together the eggs, cheddar cheese, parmesan, salt, and pepper in a mixing dish, then pour over the dough.
3. Spread the ham on top, then cut the remaining crescent roll dough into strips and place them on top of the ham. Bake for 25 minutes at 148° C.
4. Breakfast should be served with the pie.

Nutritional information: calories 400, fat 27g, fiber 7g, carbs 22g, protein 16g

Blackberry French Toast

Preparation time: 10 minutes

Cooking time: 20 minutes
Servings: 6

Ingredients:
- 407 g blackberry jam, warm
- 340 g bread loaf, cubed
- 226 g cream cheese, cubed
- 4 eggs
- 5 ml cinnamon powder
- 450 ml half and half
- 100 g brown sugar
- 5 ml vanilla extract
- Cooking spray

Preparation
1. Cooking spray your air fryer and set it to 148 degrees Celsius.
2. On the bottom, layer blueberry jam, half of the bread cubes, cream cheese, then the remaining bread.
3. Whisk together the eggs, half and half, cinnamon, sugar, and vanilla extract in a mixing bowl. Pour the bread mix on top.
4. Cook for 20 minutes before dividing amongst plates for breakfast.

Nutritional information: calories 215, fat 6g, fiber 9g, carbs 16g, protein 6g

Beans and Egg Breakfast Mix

Preparation time: 10 minutes
Cooking time: 10 minutes
Servings: 3

Ingredients:
- 2 eggs, whisked
- 3 g soy sauce
- 15 ml olive oil
- 4 garlic cloves, minced
- 85 g French beans, trimmed and sliced diagonally
- Salt and white pepper to the taste

Preparation
1. Whisk together the eggs, soy sauce, salt, and pepper in a mixing bowl.
2. Preheat your air fryer to 160°C before adding the oil and heating it up.
3. Brown the garlic for 1 minute.

4. After adding the French beans and egg mixture, cook for 10 minutes.
5. Serve on separate plates for breakfast.

Nutritional information: calories 182, fat 3g, fiber 6g, carbs 8g, protein 3g

Okra and Corn Salad

Preparation time: 10 minutes
Cooking time: 12 minutes
Servings: 6

Ingredients:
- 454 g okra, trimmed
- 6 scallions, chopped
- 3 green bell peppers, chopped
- Salt and black pepper to the taste
- 30 ml olive oil
- 5 g sugar
- 794 g canned tomatoes, chopped
- 128 g con

Preparation
1. In a pan large enough to fit your air fryer, heat the oil over medium-high heat, then add the scallions and bell peppers, swirl, and cook for 5 minutes.
2. Stir in the okra, salt, pepper, sugar, tomatoes, and corn before frying for 7 minutes at 182 degrees C in the air fryer.
3. While the okra combination is still hot, serve it on plates.

Nutritional information: calories 152, fat 4g, fiber 3g, carbs 18g, protein 4g

APPETIZER AND SNACKS

Air Fryer Carrot Fries
Prep Time 10 min
Cook Time 14 min
Serving: 2-3

Ingredients
- 4-5 carrots, peeled
- 10 ml cornstarch
- 2.5 ml parsley
- 2.5 ml garlic powder
- 1.25 ml salt
- 15 ml olive oil
- 3 g grated parmesan

Preparation
1. Preheat the air fryer to 204 degrees Celsius.
2. Carrots should be peeled. Cut each carrot in half to make shorter fries. Then, lengthwise, cut them in half, then again lengthwise. They should all be around the same size for even cooking.
3. In a small mixing bowl, combine the cornstarch, parsley, garlic powder, and salt. Drizzle olive oil over your carrots and serve. Then, toss the carrots in the spice to coat evenly.
4. Place them in a single layer in your air fryer basket. Air fried for 13-15 minutes, or until fork soft but still holding their shape when held up to the light. Allow them to rest for a few minutes to crisp up even more. Arrange them on a plate and sprinkle with parmesan cheese. Serve immediately.

Nutrition Information: Calories: 79 Fat: 5g Carbs: 8g fiber: 2g Sugar: 3g Protein: 1g

Coconut Chicken Bites
Preparation time: 10 minutes
Cooking time: 13 minutes
Servings: 4

Ingredients:
- 10 ml garlic powder
- 2 eggs
- Salt and black pepper to the taste
- 89 g panko bread crumbs
- 53 g coconut, shredded
- Cooking spray
- 8 chicken tenders

Preparation
1. In a mixing bowl, combine eggs, salt, pepper, and garlic powder.

2. In a separate dish, stir together the coconut and panko.
3. Dip the chicken tenders in the egg mixture and then in the coconut mixture.
4. Spray the chicken bits with cooking spray, place them in the air fryer basket, and cook at 176° C for 10 minutes.
5. Arrange them on a platter to serve as an appetizer.

Nutritional information: calories 252, fat 4, fiber 2, carbs 14, protein 24

Air Fryer Jalapeno Poppers
Prep Time 15 minutes
Cook Time 12 minutes
Servings 4

Ingredients
- 6-8 jalapenos sliced lengthwise with seeds removed
- 142 g cream cheese softened
- 2 pieces cooked crumbled bacon
- 1 garlic clove finely minced
- 3 g chives minced
- 11 g grated Parmesan cheese
- 1.25 ml salt more to taste if necessary
- 33 g panko breadcrumbs
- 14 g melted butter

Preparation
1. Combine the breadcrumbs and melted butter in a separate bowl.
2. Blend the remaining ingredients in a mixing bowl and well combine.
3. Fill each jalapeo half with the ingredients until it is completely gone.
4. On top, buttered breadcrumbs.
5. Cook the jalapenos in the air fryer basket in a single layer for 10-12 minutes, or until the breadcrumbs are golden brown and crisped. (You may need to air fry them in two batches.)
6. Dress with Ranch or Cajun remoulade dressing and serve.

Nutritional information Calories: 230kcal Carbs: 7g Protein: 5g Fat: 20g Fiber: 1g Sugar: 2g

Shrimp Muffins
Preparation time: 10 minutes
Cooking time: 26 minutes
Servings: 6

Ingredients:

- 1 spaghetti squash, peeled and halved
- 28 g mayonnaise
- 28 g mozzarella, shredded
- 227 g shrimp, peeled, cooked, and chopped
- 126 g cups panko
- 5 ml parsley flakes
- 1 garlic clove, minced
- Salt and black pepper to the taste
- Cooking spray

Preparation
1. Cook squash halves in an air fryer for 16 minutes at 176°C, then leave aside to cool and scrape flesh into a basin.
2. Combine the salt, pepper, parsley flakes, panko, shrimp, mayo, and mozzarella in a mixing bowl.
3. Spray a muffin pan that fits your air fryer with cooking spray and spoon the squash and shrimp mixture into each cup.
4. Cook for 10 minutes at 182 degrees Celsius in your air fryer.
5. Serve the muffins on a platter as a snack.

Nutritional information: calories 60g, fat 2g, fiber 0.4g, carbs 4g, protein 4g

Stuffed Peppers

Preparation time: 10 minutes
Cooking time: 8 minutes
Servings: 8

Ingredients:
- 8 small bell peppers, tops cut off and seeds removed
- 15 ml olive oil
- Salt and black pepper to the taste
- 100 g goat cheese, cut into 8 pieces

Preparation
1. In a mixing dish, combine the cheese, oil, salt, and pepper.
2. Stuff each pepper with goat cheese and cook for 8 minutes at 204° C in an air fryer basket. Place on a plate and serve as an appetizer.

Nutritional information: calories 120, fat 1g, fiber 1g, carbs 12g, protein 8g

Zucchini Cakes

Preparation time: 10 minutes
Cooking time: 12 minutes
Servings: 12

Ingredients:
- Cooking spray
- 70 g dill, chopped
- 1 egg
- 65 g whole wheat flour
- Salt and black pepper to the taste
- 1 yellow onion, chopped
- 2 garlic cloves, minced
- 3 zucchinis, grated

Preparation
1. Combine zucchini, garlic, onion, flour, salt, pepper, egg, and dill in a mixing bowl; whisk thoroughly. Form small patties from this mixture, coat with cooking spray, and cook for 6 minutes on each side at 187 degrees C.
2. Serve them as a snack right away.

Nutritional information: calories 60, fat 1g, fiber 2g, carbs 6g, protein 2g

Pumpkin Muffins

Preparation time: 10 minutes
Cooking time: 15 minutes
Servings: 18

Ingredients:
- 57 g butter
- 169 g pumpkin puree
- 20 g flaxseed meal
- 34 g flour
- 100 g sugar
- 2.5 ml nutmeg, ground
- 5 ml cinnamon powder
- 2.5 ml baking soda
- 1 egg
- 2.5 ml baking powder

Preparation
1. Combine the butter, pumpkin puree, and egg in a mixing dish.
2. Combine the flaxseed meal, flour, sugar, baking soda, baking powder, nutmeg, and cinnamon in a mixing bowl.
3. Fill a muffin tin large enough to accommodate your fryer with this. In the fryer, bake for 15 minutes at 176 degrees Celsius.
4. Serve muffins cold as a snack.

Nutritional information: calories 50, fat 3g, fiber 1g, carbs 2g, protein 2g

Stuffed Tomatoes With Spinach And Cheese

Prep Time: 20 min
Cook Time: 15 min
Servings: 4

Ingredients
- 4 Tomatoes ripe beefsteak
- 4 ml Ground Black Pepper
- 2.5 ml Kosher Salt
- 284 g Frozen Spinach thawed and squeezed dry
- 147 g garlic-and-herb Boursin cheese
- 45 ml sour cream
- 45 g Grated Parmesan Cheese finely grated

Preparation
1. Remove the tomatoes' tops. Using a small spoon, remove and discard the pulp.
2. Season the insides of the tomatoes with 2.5 mL black pepper and 1.25 mL salt. While you prepare the filling, drain the tomatoes on paper towels.
3. In a medium mixing bowl, combine the spinach, Boursin cheese, sour cream, salt and pepper, and 45 g of the grated parmesan. Stir until all of the ingredients are well combined. Divide the mixture evenly among the tomatoes.
4. Finally, sprinkle with the remaining 45 g grated parmesan.
5. Half-fill the air fryer basket with tomatoes. In the air fryer, heat the filling for 15 minutes at 176°C.

Nutritional information Calories 267kcal Carbs 10g Protein 11g Fat 21g Fiber 4g Sugar 5g

Buffalo Cauliflower Snack

Preparation time: 10 minutes
Cooking time: 15 minutes
Servings: 4

Ingredients:
- 453 g cauliflower florets
- 119 g panko bread crumbs
- 57 g butter, melted
- 60 ml buffalo sauce
- Mayonnaise for serving

Preparation
1. In a mixing bowl, combine buffalo sauce and butter.

2. Coat cauliflower florets in this mixture, then in panko bread crumbs.
3. Cook for 15 minutes at 176 degrees Celsius in the basket of your air fryer.
4. Serve with mayonnaise on the side on a plate.

Nutritional information: calories 241, fat 4, fiber 7, carbs 8, protein 4

Roasted Garlic

Prep time 5 minutes
Cook Time: 20 minutes
Serving: 12 cloves (1 per serving)

Ingredients
- 1 medium head garlic
- 10 ml avocado oil

Preparation
1. Remove the garlic skin but leave the cloves alone. Remove 1/4 of the garlic head, exposing the clove tips.
2. To finish, drizzle with avocado oil. Wrap the garlic head completely in a thin layer of aluminum foil. Fill half of the air fryer basket with it.
3. Set the air fryer to 204°C set the timer to 20 minutes. If your garlic head is smaller, check it after 15 minutes.
4. The garlic should be golden brown and extremely tender when done.
5. The cloves should easily come out and be dispersed or chopped when ready to serve. Refrigerate for 5 days in an airtight container. Individual cloves can also be frozen on a baking sheet before being placed in a freezer-safe storage bag.

Nutritional information Calories: 11 Protein: 0.2 g Fiber: 0.1 g Fat: 0.7 g Carbs: 1.0 g

Empanadas

Preparation time: 10 minutes
Cooking time: 25 minutes
Servings: 4

Ingredients:
- 1 package of empanada shells
- 15 ml olive oil
- 454 g beef meat, ground
- 1 yellow onion, chopped
- Salt and black pepper to the taste
- 2 garlic cloves, minced
- 2.5 ml cumin, ground
- 56 g tomato salsa

- 1 egg yolk whisked with 15 ml water
- 1 green bell pepper, chopped

Preparation
1. Heat the oil in a skillet over medium-high heat, then brown the meat on both sides.
2. After adding the onion, garlic, salt, pepper, bell pepper, and tomato salsa, cook for 15 minutes.
3. Empanada shells should be filled with cooked meat, brushed with egg wash, and sealed.
4. Place them in the air fryer's steamer basket and cook for 10 minutes at 176° C.
5. Arrange on a plate as an appetiser.

Nutritional information: calories 274, fat 17g, fiber 14g, carbs 20g, protein 7g

Spinach Balls

Preparation time: 10 minutes
Cooking time: 7 minutes
Servings: 30

Ingredients:
- 57 g butter, melted
- 2 eggs
- 250 g flour
- 454 g spinach
- 50 g feta cheese, crumbled
- 1.25 ml g nutmeg, ground
- 30 g parmesan, grated
- Salt and black pepper to the taste
- 15 ml onion powder
- 15 g whipping cream
- 5 ml garlic powder

Preparation
1. In a blender, combine the spinach, butter, eggs, flour, feta cheese, parmesan, nutmeg, whipped cream, salt, pepper, onion, and garlic pepper until smooth. Place for 10 minutes in the freezer.
2. Form 30 spinach balls, place them in the air fryer basket, and cook for 7 minutes at 149° C.
3. During a party, serve as an appetizer.

Nutritional information: calories 60, fat 5g, fiber 1g, carbs 1g, protein 2g

VEGETARIAN RECIPE

Eggplant and Zucchini Mix

Preparation time: 10 minutes
Cooking time: 8 minutes
Servings: 4

Ingredients:
- 1 eggplant, roughly cubed
- 3 zucchinis, roughly cubed
- 30 ml lemon juice
- Salt and black pepper to the taste
- 5 ml thyme, dried
- 5 ml oregano, dried
- 40 g olive oil

Preparation
1. Toss eggplant with zucchinis, lemon juice, salt, pepper, thyme, oregano, and olive oil in an air fryer-safe dish, and cook at 182 degrees C for 8 minutes.
2. Serve on separate plates right away.

Nutritional information: calories 152, fat 5g, fiber 7g, carbs 19g, protein 5g

Air Fried Broccoli Salad Broccoli

Prep Time: 10 minutes
Cook Time: 7 minutes
Servings 2

Ingredients
- 213 g fresh broccoli florets
- 28 g salted butter, melted
  23 g sliced almonds
- 1/2 medium lemon

preparation
1. Place broccoli in a 6" round baking dish, drizzle with butter, stir with almonds, and place in the air fryer basket.
2. Set the air fryer temperature to 193°C and the timer for 7 minutes.
3. Halfway through the cooking time, stir.
4. When the timer goes off, zest the lemon onto the broccoli and squeeze the juice into the pan; toss and serve warm.

Nutritional information calorie 215 protein 6.4 g fiber 5.0 g fat 16.3 g carbs 12.1 g sugar 3.0 g

Roasted Asparagus

Prep Time 3 mins
Cook Time 7 mins
Total Time 10 mins
Servings: 6

Ingredients

- 454 g asparagus
- 15 ml olive oil
- 11 g grated Parmesan
- 5 ml garlic powder
- 5 ml salt
- 1/2 lemon

Preparation

1. Remove the asparagus ends and place them in a mixing bowl.
2. To coat, toss the salad with the olive oil.
3. To coat the asparagus, combine the Parmesan, garlic powder, and salt.
4. Cook the asparagus for 7 minutes at 204 oC in the air fryer basket, shaking halfway through.
5. Squeeze lemon over the asparagus just before serving.

Nutritional information

Calories: 72kcal Carbohydrates: 7g Protein: 4g Fat: 4g | Saturated Fat: 1g Cholesterol: 2mg Fiber: 3g Sugar: 2g

Tomato and Basil Tart

Preparation time: 10 minutes
Cooking time: 14 minutes
Servings: 2

Ingredients:

- 1 bunch basil, chopped
- 4 eggs
- 1 garlic clove, minced
- Salt and black pepper to the taste
- 114 g cherry tomatoes, halved
- 60 g cheddar cheese, grated

Preparation

1. In a mixing bowl, combine the eggs, salt, black pepper, cheese, and basil.

2. Pour mixture into a baking dish that fits your air fryer, cover with tomatoes, and cook for 14 minutes at 160 degrees C.
3. After slicing, serve immediately.

Nutritional information: calories 140, fat 1g, fiber 1g, carbs 2g, protein 10g

Stuffed Tomatoes

Preparation time: 10 minutes
Cooking time: 15 minutes
Servings: 4

Ingredients:
- 4 tomatoes, tops cut off and pulp scooped and chopped
- Salt and black pepper to the taste
- 1 yellow onion, chopped
- 14 g butter
- 15 g celery, chopped
- 50 g mushrooms, chopped
- 7 g bread crumbs
- 162 g cottage cheese
- 1.25 ml caraway seeds
- 4 g parsley, chopped

Preparation
1. Melt the butter in a skillet over medium heat, then stir in the onion and celery for 3 minutes.
2. After adding the tomato pulp and mushrooms, cook for 1 minute more.
3. Cook for another 4 minutes, stirring frequently, after adding salt, pepper, crumbled bread, cheese, caraway seeds, and parsley.
4. Stuff tomatoes with this mixture and cook in an air fryer for 8 minutes at 176° C.
5. Place the stuffed tomatoes on plates and serve.

Nutritional information: calories 143, fat 4g, fiber 6g, carbs 4g, protein 4g

Brussels Sprouts and Butter Sauce

Preparation time: 4 minutes
Cooking time: 10 minutes
Servings: 4

Ingredients:
- 454 g Brussels sprouts, trimmed
- Salt and black pepper to the taste
- ½ cup bacon, cooked and chopped
- 15 g mustard
- 15 g butter

- 2 g dill, finely chopped

Preparation
1. Cook Brussels sprouts for 10 minutes at 176 degrees Celsius in your air fryer.
2. Melt the butter in a skillet over medium-high heat, then add the bacon, mustard, and dill and thoroughly combine.
3. Serve Brussels sprouts on plates drizzled with butter sauce.

Nutritional information: calories 162, fat 8g, fiber 8g, carbs 14g, protein 5g

Tomatoes and Bell Pepper Sauce

Preparation time: 10 minutes
Cooking time: 15 minutes
Servings: 4

Ingredients:
- 2 red bell peppers, chopped
- 2 garlic cloves, minced
- 454 g cherry tomatoes, halved
- 5 ml rosemary, dried
- 3 bay leaves
- 30 ml olive oil
- 15 ml balsamic vinegar
- Salt and black pepper to the taste

Preparation
1. Toss tomatoes in a dish with garlic, salt, black pepper, rosemary, bay leaves, half of the oil, and half of the vinegar, toss to coat, and cook for 15 minutes at 160 degrees C in an air fryer.
2. Meanwhile, mix bell peppers, a sprinkle of sea salt, black pepper, the remaining oil, and the remaining vinegar in a food processor and thoroughly blend.
3. Arrange the roasted tomatoes on plates and sprinkle with the bell pepper sauce.

Nutritional information: calories 123, fat 1g, fiber 1g, carbs 8g, protein 10g

Crispy Potatoes and Parsley

Preparation time: 10 minutes
Cooking time: 10 minutes
Servings: 4

Ingredients:
- 454 g gold potatoes, cut into wedges
- Salt and black pepper to the taste
- 30 ml olive

- Juice from ½ lemon
- 15 g parsley leaves, chopped

Preparation
1. Rub potatoes with salt, pepper, lemon juice, and olive oil before frying for 10 minutes at 176° C in an air fryer.
2. Serve on plates with parsley sprinkled on top.

Nutritional information: calories 152, fat 3g, fiber 7g, carbs 17g, protein 4g

Turnips Salad

Preparation time: 10 minutes
Cooking time: 12 minutes
Servings: 4

Ingredients:
- 567 g turnips, peeled and chopped
- 5 ml garlic, minced
- 5 ml ginger, grated
- 2 yellow onions, chopped
- 2 tomatoes, chopped
- 5 ml cumin, ground
- 5 ml coriander, ground
- 2 green chilies, chopped
- 2.5 ml turmeric powder
- 28 g butter
- Salt and black pepper to the taste
- A handful of coriander leaves, chopped

Preparation
1. Melt the butter in an air fryer-compatible pan, then add the green chilies, garlic, and ginger, mix, and cook for 1 minute.
2. Stir in the onions, salt, pepper, tomatoes, turmeric, cumin, ground coriander, and turnips, then cook for 10 minutes at 176°C in the air fryer.
3. Serve on plates garnished with fresh coriander.

Nutritional information: calories 100, fat 3g, fiber 6g, carbs 12g, protein 4g

Broccoli Crust Pizza

Prep Time: 15 minutes
Cook Time: 12 minutes
Serves 4

Ingredients
- 340 g riced broccoli, steamed and drained well
- 1 large egg
- 45 g grated vegetarian Parmesan cheese
- 45 ml low-carb Alfredo sauce
- 56 g shredded mozzarella cheese

Preparation
1. In a large mixing bowl, combine broccoli, egg, and Parmesan.
2. Fit your air fryer basket with parchment paper. Press the pizza ingredients to fit on the parchment, working in two batches if necessary. Insert the air fryer basket into the air fryer.
3. Set the air fryer to 187°C set the timer to 5 minutes.
4. When the timer goes off, the crust should be firm enough to turn. If not, increase the time by 2 minutes. Flip the pie crust over.
5. On top, Alfredo sauce and mozzarella cheese. Return the air fryer basket to the air fryer and cook for another 7 minutes, or until the cheese is brown and bubbling. Serve immediately.

Nutritional information calories: 136 protein: 9.9 g fiber: 2.3 g net carbs: 3.4 g fat: 7.6 g carbohydrates: 5.7 g sugar: 1.1 g

Baked Crispy Avocado Tacos

Prep Time 20 mins
Cook Time 10 mins
Total Time 30 mins
Servings 4

Ingredients
Salsa (can sub your favorite store bought)
- 1 cup finely chopped or crushed pineapple
- 1 roma tomato finely diced
- ½ red bell pepper finely diced
- 26 g finely diced red onion about ½ of an onion
- 1 clove garlic minced
- ½ jalapeno finely diced
- Pinch each cumin and salt

Avocado Tacos
- 1 avocado
- 35 g all purpose flour
- 1 large egg whisked
- 65 g panko crumbs diced
- Pinch each salt and pepper
- 4 flour tortillas click for recipe

Adobo Sauce
- 60 g plain yogurt

- 30 g mayonnaise
- 1.25 g lime juice
- 15 ml adobo sauce from a jar of chipotle peppers

Preparation
1. Salsa: Combine all of the Salsa ingredients (finely chop by hand or blitz in a food processor), cover, and chill.
2. Prep Avocado: Remove the pit from the avocado and cut it in half lengthwise. Cut each half of the avocado into four equal-sized pieces, then gently peel the skin off of each.
3. Prep Station: Preheat the air fryer to 190 degrees Celsius. Arrange a bowl of flour, a beaten egg, a bowl of panko with salt and pepper mixed in, and a parchment-lined baking sheet at the end of your workspace.
4. Coat: Each avocado slice should be dipped in flour, then egg, and finally panko. Air fry for 10 mins, flipping halfway through cooking, until lightly coloured, on the prepared baking sheet.
5. Sauce: While the avocados are frying, whisk together all of the Sauce ingredients.
6. Serve: Spoon salsa into a tortilla, then top with 2 avocado slices and sprinkle with sauce. Serve right away and enjoy!

Nutritional information Calories: 624kcal Carbs: 70.7g Protein: 14.1g Fat: 34.7g Fiber: 13.7g

Air Fryer Green Beans

Prep Time 2 mins
Cook Time 8 mins
Total Time 10 mins
Servings: 4

Ingredients
- 454 g fresh green beans trimmed
- 15 ml olive oil
- 11 g grated Parmesan cheese
- 5 ml garlic powder
- 5 ml salt
- 1 lemon juice of

Preparation
1. In a bowl, drizzle olive oil over the green beans. Mix in the Parmesan, garlic powder, and salt.
2. Place the green beans in an air fryer basket and cook for 8-10 minutes, or until tender.
3. Squeeze a fresh lemon over the green beans before serving and season with salt to taste.

Nutritional information Calories: 80kcal Carbs: 9g Protein: 3g Fat: 4g Fiber: 3g

FISH AND SEAFOOD

Air Fryer Lobster Tails with Lemon-Garlic Butter

Prep: 10 mins
Cook: 10 mins
Total: 20 mins
Servings: 2

Ingredients
- 2 (113 ml) lobster tails
- 56 g butter
- 5 ml lemon zest
- 1 clove garlic, grated
- salt and ground black pepper to taste
- 5 ml chopped fresh parsley
- 2 wedges lemon

Preparation
1. Preheat the air fryer to 195 degrees Celsius.
2. Butterfly lobster tails by cutting the hard outer shells and flesh with kitchen shears lengthwise. Cut to the shell bottoms but not through them. Split the tail in half. Place the lobster tails, flesh side up, in the air fryer basket.
3. In a small saucepan over medium heat, melt the butter. Warm the lemon zest and garlic for 30 seconds, or until aromatic.
4. Brush the lobster tails with 28 g of the butter mixture; remove any additional spread butter to avoid infection with raw lobster. Season the lobster to taste with salt and pepper.
5. In a preheated air fryer, cook until the lobster meat is opaque, 5 to 7 minutes.
6. Any residual butter from the skillet should be spooned over the lobster flesh. Garnish with lemon wedges and parsley.

Nutritional information
calories313; protein 18.1g; carbs 3.3g; fat 25.8g; cholesterol 128.7mg; sodium 590.4mg.

Air Fried Salmon Cakes

Prep Time: 10 min
Cook Time: 12 min
Total Time: 22 min
Servings: 4

Ingredients
- 1 (418 g.) can salmon, drained and flaked
- 2 eggs, beaten
- 28 g diced onion
- 14 g chopped fresh parsley

Preparation
1. Preheat your air fryer to 204 C for 4 minutes.
2. Combine the salmon, eggs, onion, and parsley in a medium mixing bowl. Divide into 8 groups.
3. Place the salmon cakes in the air fryer basket in a single layer and cook for 6 minutes on each side, or until an instant meat thermometer reads 71 C. Continue with the rest of the salmon cakes.
4. If desired, garnish with parsley and lemon. Have fun while serving!

Nutrition Information:
Calories: 166 Total Fat: 9gSaturated Fat: 2g Cholesterol: 129mg Sodium: 73mg Carb: 3g Fiber: 1g Sugar: 1g Protein: 16g

Air Fryer White Fish with Garlic

Prep Time 5 mins
Cook Time 12 mins
Total Time 17 mins
Servings: 2

Ingredients
- 340 g tilapia filets , or other white fish (2 filets-6 ounces each)
- 2.5 ml garlic powder
- 2.5 ml lemon pepper seasoning
- 2.5 ml onion powder , optional
- kosher salt or sea salt , to taste
- fresh cracked black pepper , to taste
- fresh chopped parsley
- lemon wedges

Preparation
1. Preheat the Air Fryer at 182°C for 5 minutes.
2. The fillets of fish should be washed and patted dry. After spraying or coating with olive oil spray, season with garlic powder, lemon pepper, and/or onion powder, salt, and pepper. Rep on the opposite side.
3. Fill the air fryer's base with perforated air fryer baking paper. Lightly spray the paper. (If you're not using a liner, spray the bottom of the air fryer basket with olive oil spray to keep the fish from sticking.)
4. Arrange the fish on top of the paper. Pair the salmon with two lemon wedges.
5. Air fried the fish for 6-12 minutes at 182°C, or until it can be flaked with a fork. The thickness of the fillets, the temperature of the fillets, and personal preference will all influence timing.

6. Serve hot, garnished with toasted lemon wedges and chopped parsley. Season with more spices or salt and pepper to taste.

Nutritional information
Calories: 169kcal Carbohydrates: 1g Protein: 34g Fat: 3g Saturated Fat: 1g Cholesterol: 85mg Fiber: 1g Sugar: 1g

Air Fryer Lemon Pepper Shrimp

Prep Time: 5 mins
Cook Time: 10 mins
Total Time: 15 mins

Ingredients
- 15 ml olive oil
- 1 lemon, juiced
- 5 g lemon pepper
- 1.25 ml g paprika
- 1.25 ml g garlic powder
- 340 g uncooked medium shrimp, peeled and deveined
- 1 lemon, sliced

Preparation
1. Preheat an air fryer to 200 degrees Celsius according the manufacturer's instructions.
2. Combine the oil, paprika, garlic powder, lemon juice, and lemon pepper in a mixing bowl. Coat the shrimp well.
3. Cook the shrimp for 6 to 8 minutes in a preheated air fryer, or until the flesh is opaque and the shrimp are vivid pink on the exterior. Serve with lemon wedges.

Nutritional information: calories 215 total fat 9g total carbohydrate 13g dietary fiber 6g protein 29g

Red Snapper

Preparation time: 30 minutes
Cooking time: 15 minutes
Servings: 4

Ingredients:
- 1 big red snapper cleaned and scored
- Salt and black pepper to the taste
- 3 garlic cloves, minced
- 1 jalapeno, chopped
- 113 g okra, chopped
- 14 g butter
- 30 ml olive oil
- 1 red bell pepper, chopped
- 30 ml white wine

- 8 g parsley, chopped

Preparation
1. In a bowl, combine the jalapeo, wine, and garlic, then spread it all over the snapper.
2. After seasoning the fish with salt and pepper, set it for 30 minutes.
3. Meanwhile, in a skillet over medium heat, melt 14 g butter, add the bell pepper and okra, mix, and cook for 5 minutes.
4. Stuff the belly of the red snapper with this mixture, parsley, and olive oil.
5. In a hot air fryer, cook for 15 minutes at 204 degrees C, turning halfway through.
6. Serve on separate plates.

Nutritional information: calories 261, fat 7g, fiber 18g, carbs 28g, protein 18g

Swordfish and Mango Salsa

Preparation time: 10 minutes
Cooking time: 6 minutes
Servings: 2

Ingredients:
- 2 medium swordfish steaks
- Salt and black pepper to the taste
- 30 ml avocado oil
- 4 g cilantro, chopped
- 1 mango, chopped
- 1 avocado, pitted, peeled, and chopped
- A pinch of cumin
- A pinch of onion powder
- A pinch of garlic powder
- 1 orange, peeled and sliced
- 8 ml balsamic vinegar

Preparation
1. Season the fish steaks with salt, pepper, garlic powder, onion powder, and cumin, then coat with half of the oil and cook for 6 minutes, flipping halfway, in the air fryer at 182 oC.
2. Meanwhile, combine the avocado, mango, cilantro, balsamic vinegar, salt, pepper, and the remaining oil in a mixing dish.
3. Serve the fish on plates beside mango salsa and orange wedges.

Nutritional information: calories 200, fat 7g, fiber 2g, carbs 14g, protein 14g

Air Fried Salmon

Preparation time: 1 hour
Cooking time: 15 minutes

Servings: 2

Ingredients:
- 2 medium salmon fillets
- 89 ml light soy sauce
- 15 ml mirin
- 5 ml water
- 89 ml honey

Preparation
1. In a mixing bowl, combine soy sauce, honey, water, and mirin. Chill for 1 hour after adding the fish.
2. Cook the salmon for 15 minutes at 182 degrees Celsius in an air fryer, turning after 7 minutes.
3. Meanwhile, heat the soy marinade in a saucepan over medium heat, stir well, and simmer for 2 minutes before removing from heat.
4. Serve the salmon with the marinade poured all over it on plates.

Nutritional information: calories 300, fat 12g, fiber 8g, carbs 13g, protein 24g

Air Fry Crunchy Cod Fillets

Prep Time: 10 mins
Cook Time: 12 mins
Total Time: 22 mins

Ingredients
- avocado oil cooking spray
- 33 g unseasoned panko bread crumbs
- 53 g stone-ground yellow cornmeal
- 6 g seasoning mix
- 5 ml paprika
- 2.5 ml salt, or to taste
- 118 ml buttermilk
- 3 (142 g) cod fillets
- 8 g all-purpose flour

Preparation
1. Make a 3-inch wide foil sling that stretches over the bottom and up the sides of a basket-style air fryer. Make a few holes in the bottom of the foil sling that match to the holes in the basket. Spray the sling with avocado oil. If you're using a shelf-style air fryer, skip this step.
2. Preheat the air fryer to 200 degrees Celsius.
3. Combine the panko crumbs, yellow cornmeal, seasoning mix, paprika, and salt in a small bowl. In a separate basin, combine the buttermilk.
4. Pat dry the fish fillets with paper towels before gently sprinkling both sides with flour. Before coating with the crumb mixture, each flour-coated fillet should be dipped in buttermilk. Place

each fillet on the foil sling or the rack of a shelf-style air fryer and coat with the crumb mixture on all sides. Spray each salmon fillet with avocado oil.
5. Cook for 10 to 12 minutes in an air fryer, or until the salmon flakes easily. The cod fillets should be removed from the air fryer using the sling and served immediately.

Nutritional information: calories 224 total fat 2g total carbohydrate 23g dietary fiber 1g total sugars 2g protein 30g

Air Fried Scallops

Prep Time 5 mins
Cook Time 6 mins
Total Time 6 mins
Servings: 2

Ingredients
- 454 g sea scallops
- 5 ml lemon pepper seasoning
- Olive oil spray
- Fresh chopped parsley, to garnish

Preparation
1. Preheat your air fryer to 204 C for 5 minutes.
2. Meanwhile, pat the scallops dry with paper towels, spritz with olive oil, and season with lemon pepper spice on both sides.
3. In the preheated air fryer basket, cook for 6 minutes at 204 C, turning halfway through.
4. Remove from the air fryer and serve with your favorite sauce.

Nutrition Information:
Calories: 314 Total Fat: 9g Saturated Fat: 1g Cholesterol: 93mg Carbohydrates: 13g Fiber: 0g Sugar: 0g Protein: 47g

Air Fried Shrimp

Prep Time 5 Mins
Cook Time 10 Mins
Total Time 15 Mins
Servings 8

Ingredients
- 25 large shrimp peeled and deveined
- 2/3 cup almond flour
- 3 eggs

- 15 ml ground black pepper
- 5 ml smoked paprika
- 5 ml lemon pepper (optional)

Preparation
1. Preheat your Air Fryer to 198 degrees Celsius. Coat the air fryer basket with nonstick cooking spray.
2. Prepare two bowls. Combine the almond flour flour, paprika, lemon pepper, and ground black pepper in a mixing bowl. Combine the beaten eggs in the second dish.
3. Dip the shrimp in the egg mixture, then back into the almond flour mixture. Place on a wire rack until all of the shrimp are used.
4. Cook the shrimp in a single layer in the prepared air fryer basket for 10-12 minutes at 198 C. Flip the shrimp halfway through.
5. Remove from the air fryer until golden brown and serve right away.

Nutritional information
Calories: 98kcal Carbohydrates: 1g Protein: 8g Fat: 7g Saturated Fat: 1g Cholesterol: 109mg Fiber: 1g Sugar: 1g

Air-Fried Shrimp Fajitas

Prep Time: 15 mins
Cook Time: 10 mins
Total Time: 25 mins

Ingredients
- 227 g large shrimp, peeled and deveined
- 1 small onion, cut into thin strips
- 1 small green bell pepper, cut into slim strips
- 1 small red bell pepper, cut into thin strips
- cooking spray
- 8 g family-style fajita seasoning or to taste
- 10 ml lime juice
- 4 flour tortillas, warmed

Preparation
1. Heat the air fryer to 200 degrees Celsius for three minutes.
2. Combine the shrimp, onion, and bell peppers in a mixing basin. Spray sparingly with oil spray. Combine the shrimp mixture and fajita spice in a mixing bowl. Place in an air fryer basket.
3. Air fried for eight minutes. Squeeze some lime juice over the shrimp mixture. Serve with warm tortillas as quickly as possible.

Nutritional information: calories 580 total fat 13g total carbohydrate 84g dietary fiber 7g total sugars 7g protein 32g

POULTRY RECIPE

Air Fryer Shredded Chicken

Prep Time 10 mins
Cook Time 45 mins
Total Time 55 mins
Servings: 4

Ingredients
- 1 Whole Chicken
- 15 ml Extra Virgin Olive Oil
- 15 ml Italian Seasoning
- Salt & Pepper

Preparation
1. Cook the entire chicken. Tie the chicken legs together and place it, breast side up, in the air fryer basket. After spreading half of the oil to all visible skin, season with salt, pepper, and Italian seasoning or mixed herbs.
2. The chicken was air fried for 25 minutes at 180 degrees Celsius before being flipped over, oiled, and seasoned again. Then, air fried for another 20 minutes at the same temperature.
3. Allow the chicken to cool before shredding it with your hands from the carcass. Remove all of the shredded chicken's little bones.
4. Fill containers for the fridge or freezer, or use in a recipe that asks for rotisserie chicken leftovers.

Nutritional information Calories: 444 Carbs: 1g Protein: 36g Fat: 32g Fiber: 1g Sugar: 1g

Paleo Baked Chicken Nuggets in the Air Fryer

Prep Time 10 mins
Cook Time 15 mins
Total Time 25 mins
Servings 4

Ingredients
- 454 g Free-range boneless, skinless chicken breast
- Pinch sea salt
- 5 ml Sesame oil
- 28 g Coconut flour
- 2.5 ml Ground ginger
- 4 Egg whites
- 90 ml Toasted sesame seeds
- Cooking spray of choice

For the dip:

- 30 ml Natural creamy almond butter
- 20 ml Coconut aminos (or GF soy sauce)
- 15 ml Water
- 10 ml Rice vinegar
- 5 ml Sriracha, or to taste
- 2.5 ml Ground ginger
- 2.5 ml Monk Fruit (omit for whole30)

Preparation
1. Preheat your air fryer for 10 minutes at 204 degrees Celsius.
2. While the air fryer heats up, cut the chicken into 1 inch nuggets, pat dry, and place in a bowl. Toss with the sesame oil and salt until evenly coated.
3. In a large Ziploc bag, combine the coconut flour and ground ginger. Shake the chicken until it is well coated.
4. Swirl the egg whites and chicken nuggets together in a large mixing basin until fully coated.
5. Half-fill a large Ziploc bag with sesame seeds. Shake any excess egg from the chicken before putting the nuggets to the bag and shaking until completely covered.
6. Cooking spray thoroughly coat the mesh air fryer basket. Place the nuggets in the basket, taking care not to crowd them or they will become soggy. Spritz lightly with cooking spray.
7. 6 minutes in the air fryer, spray cooking spray on both sides of each nugget. Cook for 5-6 minutes more, or until the inside is no longer pink and the outside is crispy.
8. While the nuggets are frying, whisk together the sauce ingredients in a medium mixing basin until smooth.
9. Serve the nuggets alongside the dip..

Nutritional information Calories 286 Carbs 10.3g Protein 29.9g Fat 11.6g Fiber 5g Sugar: 1.5g

Best Air Fryer Chicken Fajitas Recipe

Prep Time 10 minutes
Cook Time 15 minutes
Total Time 25 minutes
Servings: 4

Ingredients
- 454 g Boneless, skinless chicken breast
- 15 ml olive oil
- 15 ml fajita seasoning
- 2 bell peppers seeded and thinly sliced
- 1 big onion, thinly sliced
- 15 g chopped fresh cilantro
- one jalapeno pepper, seeded and thinly sliced (optional)
- 15 ml lime juice
- 8 (6 inches) tortillas (your favorite) warmed

- Desired toppings

Preparation
1. In a large zip-top plastic bag or large mixing bowl, add the chicken strips, olive oil, fajita seasoning, bell pepper, and onion. Begin coating after closing the bag. Refrigerate for at least 30 minutes and up to 8 hours before serving.
2. Preheat the air fryer for 5 minutes at 198°C.
3. Cook for 15 minutes, or until the chicken is cooked through and the vegetables are tender, in the air fryer basket. Halfway through, shake the basket.
4. Combine the cooked chicken, jalapeo, cilantro, and lime juice in a medium mixing basin. Serve with tortillas of your choice and your preferred toppings.

Nutrition Information: Calories: 240 Fat: 8g Carbs: 5g Fiber: 1g Sugar: 2g Protein: 36g

Air Fryer Lemon Pepper Wings

Prep Time 5 mins
Cook Time 25 mins
Total Time 30 mins
Serving: 4

Ingredients
- 680 g chicken wings, drumettes and flats separated and tips discarded
- 10 ml McCormick lemon pepper seasoning
- 1.25 ml cayenne pepper

For The Lemon Pepper Sauce
- 43 g butter
- 5 ml McCormicks lemon pepper seasoning
- 5 ml honey

Preparation
1. Preheat your air fryer to 193 degrees Celsius.
2. Lemon pepper and cayenne pepper season the chicken wings.
3. Fill the air fryer only halfway with lemon pepper wings. Cook, shaking halfway through, for 20-22 minutes.
4. Cook for a further 3-5 minutes at 204 degrees Celsius to get a nice crispy exterior on the chicken wings.
5. While the chicken wings are cooking, mix the melted butter, additional lemon pepper spice, and honey in a dish.
6. Remove the air fryer chicken wings and coat with the lemon honey sauce.

Nutrition Information: Calories: 462 Fat: 36.2g carbs: 2g fiber: 0g sugar: 1g protein: 31.2g

Air Fryer Cheesy Bacon Hasselback Chicken

Prep Time: 10 mins
Cook Time: 15 mins
Total Time: 25 mins
Servings: 3

Ingredients
- 3 chicken breasts skinless, boneless
- 113 g. cream cheese 1/2 block
- 56 g colby jack cheese shredded
- 56 g pepper jack cheese shredded
- 60 g cheddar cheese shredded
- 56 g cooked bacon chopped
- 30 g spinach fresh, chopped
- 5 ml. garlic minced
- 5 ml. smoked paprika
- 2.5 ml. salt
- 2.5 ml. pepper
- 112 g bocconcini mini mozzarella balls

Preparation
1. Make 6 slits across the top of each chicken breast, but don't cut all the way through.
2. In a mixing bowl, thoroughly combine all of the remaining ingredients, except the bocconcini.
3. Fill each slit with the cheese mixture, then top with the bocconcini balls.
4. Before placing each chicken breast in the air fryer basket, brush it with olive oil or nonstick cooking spray. Place the basket in your air fryer.
5. For 15 minutes, preheat the air fryer to 182°C. Check for doneness; if not completely cooked, continue to cook for another minute or two.

Nutritional information Calories: 762kcal Carbs: 5g Protein: 75g Fat: 48g Fiber: 1g Sugar: 2g

Chicken and Black Olives Sauce

Preparation time: 10 minutes
Cooking time: 8 minutes
Servings: 2

Ingredients:
- 1 chicken breast cut into 4 pieces
- 30 ml olive oil
- 3 garlic cloves, minced

For the sauce:
- 180 g black olives, pitted
- Salt and black pepper to the taste
- 30 ml olive oil

- 15 g parsley, chopped
- 15 ml lemon juice

Preparation
1. In a food processor, combine olives, salt, pepper, 30 mL olive oil, lemon juice, and parsley until smooth. Transfer to a mixing basin.
2. Season the chicken with salt and pepper, massage with the oil and garlic, and cook for 8 minutes in a preheated air fryer at 187 degrees C.
3. Place the chicken on plates and cover with the olive sauce.

Nutritional information: calories 270, fat 12g, fiber 12g, carbs 23g, protein 22g

Broccoli Cheddar Chicken Fritters

Prep Time 10 minutes
Cook Time 10 minutes
Servings 8 fritters

Ingredients
- 454 g boneless skinless chicken thighs, cut into small pieces
- 2 large eggs
- 5 ml garlic powder
- 63 g all-purpose flour
- 235 g shredded cheddar cheese
- 142 g broccoli florets, steamed and chopped fine
- salt & pepper to taste
- Olive oil

Preparation
1. In a large mixing bowl, combine the bite-size chicken pieces, garlic powder, eggs, almond flour, shredded cheese, broccoli, salt, and pepper.
2. Gently fold in.
3. Fill a GREASED basket halfway with batter. Make uniform-sized fritters in your air fryer. The size of your air fryer will decide how many fritters you create. Use the back of a spoon to flatten them.
4. Preheat your air fryer to 204° C and cook for 8 minutes.
5. Cook for 2 minutes on the opposite side.
6. If you produce thicker fritters, the cooking time will need to be extended. Always check for doneness before removing from the air fryer.
7. Repeat these steps until you are runs out.

Nutritional information Calories: 166kcal Carbs: 2g Protein: 17g Fat: 11g Fiber: 1g Sugar: 1g

Chinese Stuffed Chicken

Preparation time: 10 minutes
Cooking time: 35 minutes
Servings: 8

Ingredients:
- 1 whole chicken
- 10 wolfberries
- 2 red chilies, chopped
- 4 ginger slices
- 1 yam, cubed
- 5 ml soy sauce
- Salt and white pepper to the taste
- 15 ml sesame oil

Preparation
1. Season the chicken with soy sauce and sesame oil, then stuff with wolfberries, yam cubes, chillies, and ginger.
2. Cook for 15 minutes at 182 degrees C following 20 minutes at 204 degrees C in your air fryer.
3. Carve the chicken and divide it among dishes to serve.

Nutritional information: calories 320, fat 12g, fiber 17g, carbs 22g, protein 12g

Chicken Parmesan

Preparation time: 10 minutes
Cooking time: 15 minutes
Servings: 4

Ingredients:
- 119 g panko bread crumbs
- 23 g parmesan, grated
- 1 g garlic powder
- 240 g white flour
- 1 egg, whisked
- 680 g chicken cutlets, skinless and boneless
- Salt and black pepper to the taste
- 113 g mozzarella, grated
- 473 ml tomato sauce
- 4 g basil, chopped

Preparation
1. In a mixing bowl, combine panko, parmesan, and garlic powder.
2. In a separate bowl, combine the flour and the egg.
3. Before immersing the chicken in flour, egg mixture, and panko, season it with salt and pepper.
4. Cook the chicken for 3 minutes on each side in your air fryer at 182 degrees C.

5. Place the chicken in an air fryer-safe baking dish, fill with tomato sauce, and top with mozzarella. Cook for 7 minutes at 190 degrees C in an air fryer.
6. Distribute among plates, top with basil, and serve.

Nutritional information: calories 304g, fat 12g, fiber 11g, carbs 22g, protein 15g

Chicken and Garlic Sauce

Preparation time: 10 minutes
Cooking time: 20 minutes
Servings: 4

Ingredients:
- 14 g butter, melted
- 4 chicken breasts, skin on and bone-in
- 15 ml olive oil
- Salt and black pepper to the taste
- 40 garlic cloves, peeled and chopped
- 2 thyme springs
- 60 ml chicken stock
- 8 g parsley, chopped
- 60 ml dry white wine

Preparation
1. Season the chicken breasts with salt and pepper, rub with oil, and cook for 4 minutes on each side at 182 degrees C in an air fryer. Transfer to an air fryer-safe heat-proof dish.
2. Toss in the melted butter, garlic, thyme, stock, wine, and parsley, then cook for 15 minutes at 176° C in the air fryer.
3. Serve everything on separate plates.

Nutritional information: calories 227, fat 9g, fiber 13g, carbs 22g, protein 12g

BEEF RECIPE

Air Fryer Marinated Flank Steak

Prep Time: 5
Refrigerate: 2 hours
Cook Time: 10 minutes
Total Time: 2 hours 15 minutes
Servings: 4

Ingredients
- 227 g flank steak
- 63 ml low sodium soy sauce
- 1/4 Balsamic or Italian dressing
- 5.8 grams brown sugar, regular or sugar substitute
- 10 ml garlic paste or 5 ml ground garlic
- 30 ml Worcestershire sauce
- 30 ml chili garlic sauce or 2.5 ml red pepper flakes
- 5 ml beef paste or bouillon
- salt and pepper to taste

Preparation
1. Combine the marinade ingredients in a dish or zipper-style bag. Refrigerate the steak in a bag or dish for at least 2 hours, but no more than 24 hours.
2. Allow the steak to come to room temperature for about 30 minutes before removing it from the marinade when ready to cook.
3. Preheat the air fryer for 5 minutes at 204 degrees Celsius.
4. On the interior surface or grill insert, apply nonstick oil spray.
5. Cook the steak for 4 minutes on one side. Cook for 3 minutes more, then check with a meat thermometer. Cook for a further 5 minutes if required.
6. Set aside the steak for 5-10 minutes to enable the fluids to redistribute. Cut against the grain to serve.

Nutritional information
Calories 256 Fat 10.2g Cholesterol 85mg Sodium 1486.8mg Carbohydrate 7.2g Dietary Fiber 0.1g Sugars 4.8g Protein 31.7g

Air Fryer Roast Beef

Prep Time 5 Minutes
Cook Time 40 Minutes
Additional Time 30 Minutes

Total Time 1 Hour 15 Minutes
Servings: 4-6

Ingredients
- 907 g roast beef (top roast)
- 15 ml olive oil
- 10 ml salt
- 10 ml pepper

Preparation
1. Remove the beef roast from the refrigerator and brush it with oil before seasoning with salt and pepper.
2. Allow 30 minutes for the beef roast to come to room temperature.
3. Preheat your air fryer to 193 degrees Celsius.
4. Cook the roast beef in the air fryer for 40-42 minutes, flipping every 15 minutes.
5. Remove the roast beef from the air fryer 1 degree below the desired temperature, put aside for at least 10 minutes, and serve!

Nutrition Information:
Calories: 195 total Fat: 7g saturated Fat: 2g cholesterol: 77mg sodium: 1995mg carbohydrates: 1g fiber: 0g sugar: 0g protein: 28g

Crispy Beef and Broccoli Stir-Fry

Prep Time: 1 hour
Cook Time: 20 minutes
Servings: 2

Ingredients
- 227 g sirloin steak, thinly sliced
- 30 ml soy sauce (or liquid aminos)
- 1.25 ml grated ginger
- 1.25 ml finely minced garlic
- 15 ml coconut oil
- 142 g broccoli florets
- 1.25 ml crushed red pepper
- 0.6 ml xanthan gum
- 2.5 ml sesame seeds

Preparation
1. In a large mixing bowl or storage bag, combine the meat, soy sauce, ginger, garlic, and coconut oil to marinate. Allow to marinate for 1 hour in the refrigerator.
2. Place the meat in the air fryer basket after removing it from the marinade.

3. Set the Air fryer to 160°C and the timer to 20 minutes.
4. Shake the frying basket with broccoli and red pepper after 10 minutes.
5. In a pan over medium heat, bring the marinade to a boil, then reduce to a simmer. After adding the xanthan gum, allow to thicken.
6. When the timer on the air fryer goes off, quickly pour the fryer basket onto the skillet and stir it around. Optional sesame seeds Serve immediately.

Nutritional information
Calories: 342 Protein: 27.0 g Fiber: 2.7 g Net Carbohydrates: 6.9 g Fat: 18.9 g Sodium: 418 mg Carbohydrates: 9.6 g Sugar: 1.6 g

Classic Mini Meatloaf

Prep Time: 10 minutes
Cook Time: 25 minutes
Serves 6

Ingredients
- 454 g ground beef
- 1/4 medium yellow onion, peeled and diced
- 1/2 medium green bell pepper, seeded and diced
- 1 large egg
- 21 g blanched finely ground almond flour
- 15 ml Worcestershire sauce
- 2.5 ml garlic powder
- 5 ml dried parsley
- 28 g tomato paste
- 60 ml water
- 15 ml powdered erythritol

Preparation
1. In a large mixing bowl, combine ground beef, onion, pepper, egg, and almond flour. Season with garlic powder and parsley and pour in the Worcestershire sauce. Mix until well combined.
2. Bake in two (4") loaf pans after dividing the batter in half.
3. In a small bowl, combine the tomato paste, water, and erythritol. Each loaf should be topped with half of the mixture.
4. Place bread pans in the air fryer basket in batches as needed.
5. Set the temperature of the air fryer to 176°C and the timer for 25 minutes, or until the internal temperature reaches 82°C.
6. Serve immediately.

Nutritional information
Per Serving Calories: 170 Protein: 14.9 g Fiber: 0.9 g Net Carbohydrates: 2.6 g Sugar Alcohol: 1.5 g Fat: 9.4 g Sodium: 85 mg Carbohydrates: 5.0 g Sugar: 1.5 g

Keto Meatballs With Almond Flour

Prep Time 2 hrs
Cook Time 12 mins
Total Time 2 hrs 12 mins

Ingredients

For the meatballs
- 1 kg (2.2 pounds) ground beef (or half pork half beef)
- 1 egg
- 1/2 tablespoon salt
- 10 ml freshly ground black pepper
- 10 ml oregano
- 5 ml basil
- 5 ml thyme
- 2.5 ml chili flakes
- 1 medium onion (~ 115 grams)
- 6 to 8 crushed garlic cloves
- 15 ml olive oil

For the almond flour panade
- 200 grams beef stock
- 15 ml unflavored powdered gelatin
- 75 grams almond flour

Preparation

Almond flour panade
1. (Begin this step early to allow the gelatin to harden) Fill a medium bowl halfway with heated stock and add one spoonful of gelatin. Allow a few minutes for the flower to blossom. With a fork, combine the gelatin. If it isn't totally dissolved, put it in the microwave for a few seconds at a time until it's completely liquid. Do not bring the mixture to a boil.
2. Mix in the almond flour well with the dissolved gelatin.
3. Refrigerate it until it is firm (about 2 hours)
4. Cut the firm gelatin into thin slices with a knife and smash it with a fork until it forms a crumble.

Keto meatballs
1. Chop the onion finely and smash the garlic cloves in a saucepan with one tablespoon of olive oil. Cook over medium heat until transparent, then reduce to low heat and continue to cook until they are a deep golden brown colour. Allow them to cool.
2. Combine your ground meat of choice, 1 egg, 7.5 mL of salt (or to taste), spices, the almond flour panade, and the sauteed onion and garlic.
3. Shape the meatballs using your hands. One batch yields around 24 ping-pong-sized meatballs. Press them lightly, just enough to preserve the form.
4. Preheat the air fryer to 200 degrees Celsius. Spread the meatballs in a single layer in the basket, leaving some space between them for the hot air to circulate.

5. Cook each batch of meatballs for 10 to 12 minutes, or until lightly browned and cooked through (add 4-5 minutes if cooking from frozen).

Nutrition Information:
Calories: 330 total Fat: 17.4g carbohydrates: 5.1g net Carbohydrates: 3.5g fiber: 1.7g sugar: 1.6g protein: 38.4g

Tender Air Fryer Steak with Garlic Mushrooms

Prep Time 5 mins
Cook Time 15 mins
Total Time 20 mins
Servings: 2

Ingredients
- 15 ml Avocado Oil
- 454 g Ribeye Steaks *Note 1
- 473 g Halved Fresh Mushrooms
- 2.5 ml Salt
- 2.5 ml Black Pepper
- 28 g Unsalted Butter (Melted)
- 3 Cloves Minced Garlic
- 1.25 g Red Pepper Flakes (Optional)
- Chopped Parsley (Optional Garnish)

Preparation
1. Preheat your Air Fryer at 204°C for 4 minutes.
2. Pat the steaks dry before cutting them into 1/2" cubes. In a large mixing bowl, combine the steak cubes.
3. In a large mixing bowl, combine the cubed steak and cut fresh mushrooms in half.
4. In a large mixing bowl, combine the steak chunks and mushrooms with the melted butter, garlic, salt, pepper, and red pepper flakes.
5. Place the mixture in an air fryer basket in an even, non-overlapping layer. (Depending on your AirFryer model, you may need to cook in batches.)
6. The steak and mushrooms were air fried for 7-15 minutes, turning twice throughout that period. Check the steak after 7 minutes to see whether it's done to your liking. If it's still too pink, keep cooking.
7. Garnish with parsley and serve immediately for the best flavor and texture.

Nutritional information
Calories: 663kcal Carbohydrates: 5g Protein: 49g Fat: 51g Saturated Fat: 22g Cholesterol: 168mg Sodium: 707mg Fiber: 1g Sugar: 2g

Garlic and Bell Pepper Beef

Preparation time: 30 minutes

Cooking time: 30 minutes
Servings: 4

Ingredients:
- 312 g steak fillets, sliced
- 4 garlic cloves, minced
- 30 ml olive oil
- 1 red bell pepper, cut into strips
- Black pepper to the taste
- 12 g sugar
- 30 ml fish sauce
- 10 ml corn flour
- 240 ml beef stock
- 4 green onions, sliced

Preparation
1. Combine beef, oil, garlic, black pepper, and bell pepper in an air fryer-safe pan; mix, cover, and refrigerate for 30 minutes.
2. Cook for 14 minutes at 182 degrees Celsius in your preheated air fryer.
3. In a bowl, combine the sugar and fish sauce; pour over the meat and continue to cook for 7 minutes at 182 degrees C.
4. Simmer for 7 minutes at 187 degrees C after adding the stock, corn flour, and green onions.
5. Serve everything on separate plates.

Nutritional information: calories 343, fat 3, fiber 12, carbs 26, protein 38

Flavored Rib Eye Steak

Preparation time: 10 minutes
Cooking time: 20 minutes
Servings: 4

Ingredients:
- 907 g rib eye steak
- Salt and black pepper to the taste
- 15 ml olive oil

For the rub:
- 45 ml sweet paprika
- 30 ml onion powder
- 30 ml garlic powder
- 12 g brown sugar
- 30 ml oregano, dried
- 15 ml cumin, ground
- 15 ml rosemary, dried

Preparation
1. Combine paprika, onion and garlic powder, sugar, oregano, rosemary, salt, pepper, and cumin in a mixing bowl; stir and massage this mixture over the steak.
2. Season with salt and pepper, rub with oil again, and cook at 204° C for 20 minutes, flipping halfway through.
3. Transfer the steak to a chopping board, slice it, and serve with a side salad.

Nutritional information: calories 320, fat 8, fiber 7, carbs 22, protein 21

Steaks and Scallops

Preparation time: 10 minutes
Cooking time: 14 minutes Servings: 2

Ingredients:
- 10 sea scallops
- 2 beef steaks
- 4 garlic cloves, minced
- 1 shallot, chopped
- 30 ml lemon juice
- 8 g parsley, chopped
- 3 g basil, chopped
- 2 g lemon zest
- 57 g butter
- 59 g veggie stock
- Salt and black pepper to the taste

Preparation
1. Season the steaks with salt and pepper, lay them in the air fryer, and cook for 10 minutes at 182 degrees C before transferring to a fryer-compatible pan.
2. Simmer for 4 minutes at 182 degrees C after adding the shallot, garlic, butter, stock, basil, lemon juice, parsley, lemon zest, and scallops.
3. Serve the scallops and steaks on separate dishes.

Nutritional information: calories 150, fat 2, fiber 2, carbs 14, protein 17

Chorizo and Beef Burger

Prep Time: 10 minutes
Cook Time: 15 minutes
Servings: 4

Ingredients
- 340 g ground beef

- 113 g Mexican-style ground chorizo
- 13 g chopped onion 5 slices pickled jalapeños, chopped
- 10 ml chili powder
- 5 ml minced garlic
- 1.25 ml cumin

Preparation
1. In a large mixing bowl, combine all of the ingredients. Divide the mixture into four halves and shape it into four burger patties.
2. Place the burger patties in the air fryer basket, working in batches if necessary.
3. Set the air fryer to 190°C set the timer to 15 minutes.
4. Flip the patties halfway through cooking time.
5. Serve immediately.

Nutritional information
Per Serving Calories: 291 Protein: 21.6 g Fiber: 0.9 g Net Carbohydrates: 3.8 g Fat: 18.3 G Sodium: 474 mg Carbohydrates: 4.7 g Sugar: 2.5 g

Greek Beef Meatballs Salad

Preparation time: 10 minutes
Cooking time: 10 minutes
Servings: 6

Ingredients:
- 60 ml milk
- 482 g beef, ground
- 1 yellow onion, grated
- 5 bread slices, cubed
- 1 egg, whisked
- 15 g parsley, chopped
- Salt and black pepper to the taste
- 2 garlic cloves, minced
- 7.5 g mint, chopped
- 12 ml oregano, dried
- 15 ml olive oil
- Cooking spray
- 198 g cherry tomatoes, halved
- 30 g baby spinach
- 22 ml lemon juice
- 207 ml Greek yogurt

Preparation
1. Cover shredded bread with milk and soak for a few minutes before squeezing and transferring to another basin.
2. Stir in the beef, egg, salt, pepper, oregano, mint, parsley, garlic, and onion, and shape the mixture into medium meatballs.

3. Spray them with frying spray, then set them in your air fryer for 10 minutes at 187° C.
4. In a salad bowl, combine the spinach, cucumber, and tomato.
5. Serve with the meatballs, oil, salt, pepper, lemon juice, and yoghurt.

Nutritional information: calories 200, fat 4, fiber 8, carbs 13, protein 27

PORK AND LAMB RECIPE

Easy Air Fryer Pork Chops

Prep Time: 5 mins
Cook Time: 8 mins
Additional Time: 5 mins
Total Time: 18 Minutes
Servings: 4

Ingredients
- 4 boneless pork chops ¾-1 inch thick
- 30 ml olive oil
- 15 ml brown sugar
- 5 ml dried thyme
- 5 ml dried mustard
- 5 ml garlic powder
- 2.5 ml kosher salt or coarse sea salt
- 2.5 ml tsp fresh ground pepper

Preparation
1. Preheat the air fryer at 204°C for 5 minutes.
2. While the air fryer is heating up, drizzle or brush the oil on both sides of the pork chops.
3. Combine the sugar, spices, salt, and pepper in a small bowl and sprinkle on both sides of the pork chops.
4. Place the pork chops in a single layer in the air fryer basket and return to the frying.
5. Preheat the air fryer for 8 minutes at 204°C.
6. Halfway through, flip the pork chops.
7. After the timer goes off, remove the pork chops from the air fryer and place them on a plate. The pork chops should be 63°C when tested using a meat thermometer. Add another minute or two if they aren't completed. Set aside for 5-10 minutes to rest, covered with foil.
8. Remove the foil before serving.
9. Any fluids that have escaped while the dish is resting can be preserved and served on the side.

Nutritional information
Calories: 391kcal Carbohydrates: 4g Protein: 37g Fat: 26g Saturated Fat: 8g Cholesterol: 103mg Sodium: 422mg Sugar: 3g

Air Fryer Sausage

Prep Time 1 min
Cook Time 10 mins
Total Time 11 mins
Servings: 4

Ingredients
- 4-5 Italian sausage links
- parchment paper (optional)

Preparation
1. Fill the air fryer basket halfway with sausage links. To collect any grease, line the bottom of the air fryer basket with parchment paper.
2. 10-12 minutes at 204°C, or until golden brown on the outside and juicy on the interior. Uncooked sausages should have an internal temperature of 63°C when properly cooked. Serve hot if desired.

Nutrition Information:
Calories: 323 Fat: 26g saturated Fat: 10g cholesterol: 53mg sodium: 697mg carbohydrates: 4g fiber: 0g sugar: 2g protein: 18g

Air Fryer Honey Mustard Pork Chops

Prep Time: 15 Minutes
Cook Time: 15 Minutes
Total Time: 30 Minutes
Servings: 4.

Ingredients
- 4 pork chops boneless, thick cut
- 30 ml yellow mustard
- 5 ml salt
- 5 ml black pepper
- 2.5 ml smoked paprika
- 5 ml garlic powder
- 2 Cloves garlic crushed
- 60 ml honey
- 60 ml mustard stone ground
- 60 ml mayonnaise
- 1 lemon juiced
- 15 ml olive oil
- 15 g parsley chopped for garnish

Preparation
1. Remove the pork chops from the refrigerator and allow them to come to room temperature for 15 minutes.
2. Preheat your air fryer for 5 minutes at 204 degrees Celsius.
3. Brush the pork chops with the yellow mustard. On both sides, season with salt, black pepper, and smoked paprika.
4. Allow enough room between the pork chops in your air fryer basket. Cook for 8 minutes, then flip and cook for 7 minutes more.

5. While the pork chops are cooking, make the honey mustard. In a small mixing bowl, combine honey, stone ground mustard, mayonnaise, lemon juice, olive oil, garlic powder, and crushed garlic. Whisk everything together to combine. Combine the honey mustard mixture in a pan over high heat. Cook for 5 minutes, stirring often.
6. Allow the pork chops to rest on a cutting board for 5 minutes. Serve the pork chops garnished with fresh chopped parsley and honey mustard.

Nutritional information
Calories: 430kcal Carbohydrates: 23g Protein: 31g Fat: 24g Saturated Fat: 5g Cholesterol: 96mg Sodium: 1001mg Fiber: 2g Sugar: 19g

Marinated Pork Chops and Onions

Preparation time: 24 hours
Cooking time: 25 minutes
Servings: 6

Ingredients:
- 2 pork chops
- 60 ml olive oil
- 2 yellow onions, sliced
- 2 garlic cloves, minced
- 10 g mustard
- 5 ml sweet paprika
- Salt and black pepper to the taste
- 2.5 ml oregano, dried
- 2.5 ml thyme, dried
- A pinch of cayenne pepper

Preparation
1. In a mixing bowl, combine the oil, garlic, mustard, paprika, black pepper, oregano, thyme, and cayenne.
2. Toss the onions with the meat and mustard mixture to coat, then cover and chill for 1 day.
3. Cook the beef and onion combination in an air fryer pan for 25 minutes at 182 degrees C.
4. Serve everything on separate plates.

Nutritional information: calories 384, fat 4, fiber 4, carbs 17, protein 25

Pork Chops and Green Beans

Preparation time: 10 minutes
Cooking time: 15 minutes
Servings: 4

Ingredients:
- 4 pork chops, bone-in

- 30 ml olive oil
- 4 g sage, chopped
- Salt and black pepper to the taste
- 251 g green beans
- 3 garlic cloves, minced
- 7 g parsley, chopped

Preparation
1. In a pan that fits your air fryer, combine pork chops, olive oil, sage, salt, pepper, green beans, garlic, and parsley, stir, and cook at 182 degrees C for 15 minutes.
2. Serve everything on separate plates.

Nutritional information: calories 261, fat 7, fiber 9, carbs 14, protein 20

Pulled Pork

Prep Time: 10 minutes
Cook Time: 2 1/2 hours
Serves 8

Ingredients
- 30 ml chili powder
- 5 ml garlic powder
- 2.5 ml onion powder
- 2.5 ml ground black pepper
- 2.5 ml cumin
- 1 (1.8 kg) pork shoulder

Preparation
1. In a small bowl, combine the chili powder, garlic powder, onion powder, pepper, and cumin. Rub the spice mixture into the pork shoulder's skin. Half-fill the air fryer basket with pork shoulder.
2. Set the air fryer to 176°C set the timer to 150 minutes.
3. When the pork is done, the skin will be crispy and the flesh will shred easily with two forks. The temperature inside should be at least 63 degrees Celsius.

Nutritional information
calories: 537 protein: 42.6 g fiber: 0.8 g net carbohydrates: 0.7 g fat: 35.5 g sodium: 180 mg carbohydrates: 1.5 g sugar: 0.2 g

Lamb and Spinach Mix

Preparation time: 10 minutes
Cooking time: 35 minutes

Servings: 6
Ingredients:
- 12 g ginger, grated
- 2 garlic cloves, minced
- 4 g cardamom, ground
- 1 red onion, chopped
- 454 g lamb meat, cubed
- 10 ml cumin powder
- 5 ml garam masala
- 2.5 ml chili powder
- 2.5 ml turmeric
- 10 ml coriander, ground
- 454 g spinach
- 397 g canned tomatoes, chopped

Preparation
1. In a heatproof dish that fits your air fryer, combine the lamb, spinach, tomatoes, ginger, garlic, onion, cardamom, cloves, cumin, garam masala, chile, turmeric, and coriander, and cook at 182 degrees C for 35 minutes.
2. Serve in separate bowls.

Nutritional information:
calories 160, fat 6, fiber 3, carbs 17, protein 20

Air Fryer Lamb Meatballs

Prep Time 5 minutes
Cook Time 12 minutes
Total Time 17 minutes
Servings: 4

Ingredients
- 454 g ground lamb
- 5 ml ground cumin
- 4.5 g granulated onion
- 7.5 g fresh parsley
- 1.25 ml ground cinnamon
- Salt and pepper

Preparation
1. In a large mixing bowl, combine the lamb, cumin, onion, parsley, and cinnamon. Mix until all of the ingredients are spread evenly.
2. Make 1 inch balls out of the mixture.
3. Cook the lamb meatballs in the air fryer basket at 176oC for 12-15 minutes. Shake the meatballs halfway through.

Nutrition Information:
Calories: 328 Fat: 22g Saturated Fat: 9g Cholesterol: 110mg Sodium: 95mg Carbohydrates: 1g Fiber: 0g Sugar: 0g Protein: 28g

Lamb Roast and Potatoes

Preparation time: 10 minutes
Cooking time: 45 minutes
Servings: 6

Ingredients:
- 1.8 kg lamb roast
- 1 spring rosemary
- 3 garlic cloves, minced
- 6 potatoes, halved
- 118 ml lamb stock
- 4 bay leaves
- Salt and black pepper to the taste

Preparation
1. Put potatoes in an air fryer-safe dish, add lamb, garlic, rosemary spring, salt, pepper, bay leaves, and stock, stir, and cook at 182 degrees C for 45 minutes.
2. Serve lamb slices on plates with potatoes and cooking fluids.

Nutritional information: calories 273, fat 4, fiber 12, carbs 25, protein 29

Easy Lamb Kofta

Prep Time 15 mins
Cook Time 12 mins
Total Time 27 mins
Servings 6

Ingredients
- 907 g ground lamb (can sub beef)
- 2 cloves garlic, finely minced or pressed
- 8 g chopped fresh cilantro or parsley
- 15 ml ground coriander
- 15 ml ground cumin
- 5 ml paprika
- 7.5 ml tsp salt
- 2.5 ml ground cinnamon
- 2.5 ml black pepper

Preparation

1. Before usage, soak bamboo skewers in water for at least 1 hour.
2. In a large mixing bowl, combine all of the ingredients and thoroughly combine them with your hands. Make 12 oval-shaped logs, 1 inch wide and 4 inches long. If used, thread the logs onto the skewers.
3. Cook for 10 to 12 minutes at 204ºC, or until the kofta is thoroughly browned and the center reaches at least 57ºC for medium. Allow a 5-minute break before serving.
4. Grill or bake the kofta over medium heat, turning to brown evenly.

Nutritional information

Calories: 437kcal Carbohydrates: 1.8g Protein: 37.9g Fat: 27.4g Fiber: 0.8g

DESSERT RECIPE

Chocolate Cookies

Preparation time: 10 minutes
Cooking time: 25 minutes
Servings: 12

Ingredients:
- 5 ml vanilla extract
- 113 g butter
- 1 egg
- 50 g sugar
- 250 g flour
- 85 g unsweetened chocolate chips

Preparation
1. Melt the butter in a skillet over medium heat, swirl, and cook for 1 minute.
2. Mix the egg, vanilla essence, and sugar in a mixing dish and stir thoroughly.
3. Stir in the melted butter, flour, and half of the chocolate chips.
4. Transfer to a pan that fits your air fryer, sprinkle with the remaining chocolate chips and bake for 25 minutes at 165 degrees C.
5. When it's cool enough to slice, serve.

Nutritional information: calories 230, fat 12, fiber 2, carbs 4, protein 5

Pecan Brownies

Prep Time: 10 minutes
Cook Time: 20 minutes
Servings: 6

Ingredients
- 48 g blanched finely ground almond flour
- 118 ml powdered erythritol
- 30 ml unsweetened cocoa powder
- 2.5 ml baking powder
- 57 g unsalted butter, softened
- 1 large egg
- 30 g chopped pecans
- 40 g low-carb, sugar-free chocolate chips

Preparation
1. Combine almond flour, erythritol, cocoa powder, and baking powder in a large mixing basin. Mix in the butter and egg.

2. Mix in the pecans and chocolate chips. Scoop the mixture onto a 6-inch circular baking pan. Insert the pan into the air fryer basket.
3. Set the air fryer temperature to 148°C and the timer for 20 minutes.
4. A toothpick put into the centre will come out clean when thoroughly done. Allow 20 minutes for the mixture to cool and firm up completely.

Nutritional information
Calories: 215 protein: 4.2 g fiber: 2.8 g net carbohydrates: 2.3 g sugar alcohol: 16.7 g fat: 18.9 g sodium: 53 mg carbohydrates: 21.8 g sugar: 0.6 g

Chocolate Espresso Mini Cheesecake

Prep Time: 5 minutes
Cook Time: 15 minutes
Servings: 2

Ingredients
- 50 g walnuts
- 28 g salted butter
- 30 ml granular erythritol
- 113 g full-fat cream cheese, softened
- 1 large egg
- 2.5 ml vanilla extract
- 30 ml powdered erythritol
- 10 ml unsweetened cocoa powder
- 5 ml espresso powder

Preparation
1. In a food processor, combine walnuts, butter, and granular erythritol. Pulse until the ingredients are combined and a dough forms.
2. Place the dough in the air fryer basket after pressing it onto a 4" springform pan.
3. Set the air fryer temperature to 204°C and the timer for 5 minutes.
4. When the timer goes off, remove the crust and set it aside to cool.
5. Cream cheese, egg, vanilla extract, powdered erythritol, cocoa powder, and espresso powder should be combined in a medium mixing dish until smooth.
6. Place the air fryer basket in the air fryer basket and spoon the mixture on top of the fried walnut crust.
7. Set the temperature to 148° C and the timer to 10 minutes.
8. Refrigerate for 2 hours before serving.

Nutritional information
Calories: 535 protein: 11.6 g fiber: 7.2 g net carbohydrates: 5.9 g sugar alcohol: 24.0 g fat: 48.4 g sodium: 336 mg carbohydrates: 37.1 g sugar: 5.9 g

Coconut Flour Mug Cake

Prep Time: 5 minutes
Cook Time: 25 minutes
Servings: 1

Ingredients

- 1 large egg
- 14 g coconut flour
- 30 g heavy whipping cream
- 30 ml granular erythritol
- 1.25 ml vanilla extract
- 1.25 ml baking powder

Preparation

1. Whisk the egg in a 4" ramekin, then add the remaining ingredients. Stir until completely smooth. Place the air fryer basket in the air fryer.
2. Set the air fryer temperature to 148°C and the timer for 25 minutes. When you're finished, a toothpick should come out clean. With a spoon, serve straight from the ramekin. Serve hot.

Nutritional information

Calories: 237 protein: 9.9 g fiber: 5.0 g net carbohydrates: 5.7 g sugar alcohol: 30.0 g fat: 16.4 g sodium: 213 mg carbohydrates: 40.7 g sugar: 4.2 g

Toasted Coconut Flakes

Prep Time: 5 mins
Cook Time: 3 mins
Servings: 4

Ingredients

- 93 g unsweetened coconut flakes
- 10 ml coconut oil
- 60 ml granular erythritol
- 0.6 ml teaspoon salt

Preparation

1. In a large mixing basin, toss the coconut flakes with the oil until evenly covered. Season with erythritol and salt.
2. Fill the air fryer basket halfway with coconut flakes.
3. Set the air fryer temperature to 148°C and the timer for 3 minutes.
4. When 1 minute has passed, toss the flakes. If you want a more golden coconut flake, cook for an additional minute.
5. Keep in an airtight container for up to three days.

Nutritional information

Calories: 165 protein: 1.3 g fiber: 2.7 g net carbohydrates: 2.6 g sugar alcohol: 15.0 g fat: 15.5 g sodium: 76 mg carbohydrates: 20.3 g sugar: 0.5 g

Vanilla Pound Cake

Prep Time: 10 mins
Cook Time: 25 mins
Servings: 6

Ingredients

- 96 g blanched finely ground almond flour
- 56 g salted butter, melted
- 120 ml granular erythritol
- 5 ml vanilla extract
- 5 ml baking powder
- 123 g full-fat sour cream
- 28 g full-fat cream cheese, softened
- 2 large eggs

Preparation

1. Combine almond flour, butter, and erythritol in a large mixing basin.
2. Mix in the vanilla extract, baking powder, sour cream, and cream cheese until completely blended. Mix in the eggs.
3. Fill a 6" round baking pan halfway with batter. Insert the pan into the air fryer basket.
4. Set the air fryer temperature to 148°C and the timer for 25 minutes.
5. A toothpick pushed into the centre of the cake will come out clean when it is finished. The middle should not be damp. Allow it to cool fully before moving it, otherwise the cake may crumble.

Nutritional information

Calories: 253 protein: 6.9 g fiber: 2.0 g net carbohydrates: 3.2 g sugar alcohol: 20.0 g fat: 22.6 g sodium: 191 mg carbohydrates: 25.2 g sugar: 1.5 g

Raspberry Danish Bites

Prep Time: 30 mins
Cook Time: 7 mins
Servings: 10

Ingredients

- 96 g blanched finely ground almond flour
- 5 ml baking powder
- 45 ml granular Swerve
- 56 g full-fat cream cheese, softened
- 1 large egg

- 170 g sugar-free raspberry preserves

Preparation
1. In a large mixing basin, combine all ingredients except the preserves until a moist dough forms.
2. Freeze the bowl for 20 minutes, or until the dough is cold enough to roll into a ball.
3. Roll the dough into ten balls and carefully press each one in the middle. In the middle of each ball, place 17 g preserves.
4. Cut parchment paper to fit your air fryer basket.
5. Place each Danish bite on the parchment paper, gently pressing down to flatten the bottom.
6. Set the air fryer temperature to 204°C and the timer for 7 minutes.
7. Allow to cool completely before transferring or they may collapse.

Nutritional information
Calories: 96 protein: 3.4 g fiber: 1.3 g net carbohydrates: 4.0 g sugar alcohol: 4.5 g fat: 7.7 g sodium: 76 mg carbohydrates: 9.8 g sugar: 2.4 g

Pumpkin Cookies

Preparation time: 10 minutes
Cooking time: 15 minutes
Servings: 24

Ingredients:
- 313 g flour
- 2.5 ml baking soda
- 7 g flax seed, ground
- 45 ml water
- 122 g pumpkin flesh, mashed
- 60 ml honey
- 28 g butter
- 5 ml vanilla extract
- 80 g chocolate chips

Preparation
1. In a mixing dish, combine flax seed and water, stir, and set aside for a few minutes.
2. In a separate basin, combine the flour, salt, and baking soda.
3. Combine honey, pumpkin puree, butter, vanilla essence, and flaxseed in a third bowl.
4. Stir together the flour, honey mixture, and chocolate chips.
5. Scoop 15 mL of cookie dough onto a lined baking sheet that fits your air fryer, repeat with the remaining dough, place in your air fryer, and cook at 176° C for 15 minutes.
6. Allow cookies to cool before serving.
7. Enjoy!

Nutritional information: calories 140, fat 2, fiber 2, carbs 7, protein 10

Lime Cheesecake

Preparation time: 4 hours and 10 minutes
Cooking time: 4 minutes
Servings: 10

Ingredients:
- 28 g butter, melted
- 8.4 g sugar
- 113 g flour
- 24 g coconut, shredded
- For the filling:
- 454 g cream cheese
- Zest from 1 lime, grated
- Juice from 1 lime
- 473 ml hot water
- 2 sachets of lime jelly

Preparation
1. In a mixing bowl, combine coconut, flour, butter, and sugar; blend well and press into the bottom of an air fryer pan.
2. Meanwhile, in a separate bowl, dissolve the jelly sachets in boiling water.
3. In a mixing bowl, combine cream cheese, jelly, lime juice, and zest, and stir thoroughly.
4. Spread this over the crust, then place it in the air fryer for 4 minutes at 149° C.
5. Refrigerate for 4 hours before serving.
6. Enjoy!

Nutritional information: calories 260, fat 23, fiber 2, carbs 5, protein 7

Easy Granola

Preparation time: 10 minutes
Cooking time: 35 minutes
Servings: 4

Ingredients:
- 95 g coconut, shredded
- 71 g almonds
- 75 g pecans, chopped
- 25 g sugar
- 59 g pumpkin seeds
- 66 g sunflower seeds
- 30 ml sunflower oil
- 5 ml nutmeg, ground
- 5 ml apple pie spice mix

Preparation

1. In a mixing bowl, combine almonds and pecans with pumpkin seeds, sunflower seeds, coconut, nutmeg, and apple pie spice mix.
2. Heat the oil in a pan over medium heat, then add the sugar and stir well.
3. Stir this into the nut and coconut mixture.
4. Spread mixture on a lined baking sheet that fits your air fryer, place in your air fryer, and bakes for 25 minutes at 149 degrees C.
5. Allow your granola to cool before cutting and serving.
6. Enjoy!

Nutritional information: calories 322, fat 7, fiber 8, carbs 12, protein 7

SIDE RECIPE

Herbed Tomatoes

Preparation time: 10 minutes
Cooking time: 15 minutes
Servings: 4

Ingredients:
- 4 big tomatoes, halved and insides scooped out
- Salt and black pepper to the taste
- 15 ml olive oil
- 2 garlic cloves, minced
- 2.5 ml thyme, chopped

Preparation
1. Toss endives with garlic powder, yoghurt, curry powder, salt, pepper, and lemon juice in a mixing bowl for 10 minutes before placing them in a hot air fryer at 176 degrees C.
2. Cook for 10 minutes, divide among plates and serve as a side dish.
3. Enjoy!

Nutritional information: calories 112, fat 1, fiber 3, carbs 4, protein 4

Eggplant Side Dish

Preparation time: 10 minutes
Cooking time: 10 minutes
Servings: 4

Ingredients:
- 8 baby eggplants, scooped in the center and pulp reserved
- Salt and black pepper to the taste
- A pinch of oregano, dried
- 1 green bell pepper, chopped

- 15 ml tomato paste
- 1 bunch coriander, chopped
- 2.5 ml garlic powder
- 15 ml olive oil
- 1 yellow onion, chopped
- 1 tomato chopped

Preparation
1. Heat the oil in a pan over medium heat, add the onion, stir, and cook for 1 minute.
2. Stir in salt, pepper, eggplant pulp, oregano, green bell pepper, tomato paste, garlic powder, coriander, and tomato, simmer for another 1-2 minutes, then remove from heat and set aside to cool.
3. Stuff eggplants with this mixture, place in an air fryer basket and cook for 8 minutes at 182 degrees C.
4. Divide the eggplants among plates and serve as a side dish.
5. Enjoy!

Nutritional information: calories 200, fat 3, fiber 7, carbs 12, protein 4

Onion Rings Side Dish

Preparation time: 10 minutes
Cooking time: 10 minutes
Servings: 3

Ingredients:
- 1 onion cut into medium slices and rings separated
- 125 g cups white flour
- A pinch of salt
- 1 egg
- 237 ml milk
- 5 ml baking powder
- 89 g bread crumbs

Preparation
1. Mix flour, salt, and baking powder in a basin dredge onion rings in this mixture, and lay them on a separate dish.
2. Whisk together the flour, milk, and egg.
3. Dip onion rings in this mixture, then in breadcrumbs, and cook for 10 minutes at 182 degrees C in an air fryer basket.
4. Divide among plates and serve with a steak as a side dish.
5. Enjoy!

Nutritional information: calories 140, fat 8, fiber 20, carbs 12, protein 3

Corn with Lime and Cheese

Preparation time: 10 minutes
Cooking time: 15 minutes
Servings: 2

Ingredients:
- 2 corns on the cob, husks removed
- A drizzle of olive oil
- 83 g feta cheese, grated
- 5 g sweet paprika
- Juice from 2 limes

Preparation
1. Cook at 204 degrees C for 15 minutes, flipping once, after rubbing corn with oil and paprika.
2. Divide corn among plates, cover with cheese, drizzle with lime juice, and serve as a side dish.
3. Enjoy!

Nutritional information: calories 200, fat 5, fiber 2, carbs 6, protein 6

Potato Wedges

Preparation time: 10 minutes
Cooking time: 25 minutes
Servings: 4

Ingredients:
- 2 potatoes, cut into wedges
- 15 ml olive oil
- Salt and black pepper to the taste
- 45 ml sour cream
- 30 ml sweet chili sauce

Preparation
1. Toss potato wedges with oil, salt, and pepper in a bowl, add to the air fryer basket, and cook at 182 degrees C for 25 minutes, flipping once.
2. Serve potato wedges with sour cream and chilli sauce drizzled as a side dish.
3. Enjoy!

Nutritional information: calories 171, fat 8, fiber 9, carbs 18, protein 7

Printed in Great Britain
by Amazon